# MEN OF ISSACHAR

## UNDERSTAND THE TIMES
## KNOW WHAT TO DO

## D. ERIC WILLIAMS

D. Eric Williams, *Men of Issachar: Understand The Times, Know What To Do.*

Copyright © 2011, D. Eric Williams
www.williamsbookseller.com

Printed in the United States of America

**Men of Issachar: Understand The Times, Know What To Do.** Copyright © 2011 By D. Eric Williams. All rights reserved. No part of this publication may be reproduced or distributed in any form or by any means, graphic, electronic or mechanical, including photocopying, recording, record taping, in digital form or using any other information retrieval system without the express written permission of the author.

ISBN-13: 978-1441435675
ISBN-10: 1441435670

All scripture taken from The Holy Bible, New King James Version Copyright © 1982 by Thomas Nelson, Inc. unless otherwise noted. Used with permission

To my Father
## David J. Williams
A model of servant leadership.

And for my sons
## Elijah, Ezekiel and Isaiah
For whom I hope to be.

# Contents

Chapter One:
The Crisis Of Our Time, Page 1

Chapter Two:
Men Of Issachar, Page 21

Chapter Three:
Men Of Christ, Page 44

Chapter Four:
Understand The Times, Page 62

Chapter Five:
Know What To Do, Page 95

Chapter Six:
Kingdom Practicalities, Page 116

Chapter Seven:
The Opportunity Of Our Time, Page 130

Epilogue:
Kingdom Status, Page 150

# CHAPTER 1
## THE CRISIS OF OUR TIME

*If you fall to pieces in a crisis, there wasn't much to you in the first place* (Proverbs 24:10, The Message)

No man wants to be revealed as a lightweight in the face of crisis. Nevertheless, it is difficult to avoid the label if you don't know what to do when the chips are down. Worse yet is the man who is unable to even identify the crisis; if you don't know what is going on, how in the world will you know how to respond?

The Bible tells us, *The fear of the LORD is the beginning of wisdom, And the knowledge of the Holy One is understanding* (Proverbs 9:10). If we want to recognize crisis and know what to do our beginning point must be God and his word.

### True Crisis

According to Webster's dictionary a crisis is a "decisive moment or an unstable or crucial time or state of affairs" in history. It is fashionable to suggest the early 21$^{st}$ century is a time fraught with crisis. The powers that be tell us crisis is on every side. Indeed, when crisis does not materialize as quickly or as violently as one might expect it seems civil leadership is not averse to creating one.

Yet, we *are* in the midst of crisis. The situation we face today is not economic, environmental, political or sociological. Instead, it is a crisis of leadership at the most elementary level. It is a crisis requiring a dramatic cultural shift in order to correct the course of history. As things now stand we are headed for disaster. Even today, we are experiencing the slow unfolding of disaster all around us.

We know we are in the midst of crisis because the signs of the problem are everywhere. For instance, we see it in the breakdown of families in our nation. Statistics tell us that one third of all the marriages in America will end in divorce (datum that applies to Christian marriages as well according to research conducted by Barna Group). The number of illegitimate births is high and is rising. As a result, an increasing number of children are raised without male leadership. According to fathermag.com,

> 63% of teen suicides come from fatherless homes, 90% of all runaways and homeless children come from fatherless homes, 80% of rapists come from fatherless homes, 85% of children with behavioral problems come from fatherless homes, 71% of all high school dropouts come from fatherless homes, 75% of all adolescent patients in chemical abuse centers come from fatherless homes, and 85% of all youths in prison come from fatherless homes.

It is not just single parent households headed by a woman that suffer from a father deficit. Many families are essentially fatherless since the man of the house fails to shoulder his responsibilities. This is a problem in Christian homes and non-christian homes alike.

*The Crisis Of Our Time*

Although the crisis is not political or economic, symptoms of the problem are seen in the leftist tilt of our civil government and in the difficult economic times we face. Furthermore, the church is of no real consequence in society and this impotence is likewise reflected in a nation morally adrift.

The reason for the crisis? In short, we have arrived at this point because Christian men fail to lead coupled with a willingness on the part of secular humanists to fill the leadership vacuum. Indeed, militant humanism rules the roost in the United States and around the world. The failure of Christian men is an act of rebellion against the most high God and this attitude has infected all of society.

It may seem to be an over statement to suggest that our familial, political, economic, ecclesiastical, environmental and societal problems all stem from the same source. But to say otherwise is to say the kingdom of God is restricted to personal piety or perhaps to the limited activity of charitable church work. In reality, the Body of Christ sets the agenda for the world. Therefore, when Christian men fail to lead in the family, church and community we see the whole of society affected. Over the last several generations the church has withdrawn from society and focused on meeting the "felt needs" of its increasingly feminine population until the rapture comes. The result of that self-centered retreat from duty on the part of Christian men is in evidence all around us.

### *Family Crisis*

The Bible says men are given the responsibility to exercise leadership in their own homes. When they fail to do so, they produce a household full of ungodly people. I am not suggesting everyone in the family will become a drug addled violent offender if a Christian man fails to lead. Nevertheless, he will produce people who are fundamentally the same as the non-Christian. If a Christian man does not take headship in his own home his wife will not blossom in her calling and will fail to find security in submission to her husband. As a result she will often adopt the militant feminist ideology of the world, without even realizing it is taking place. Furthermore, poorly led, the children will turn their back on the kingdom of God and embrace worldly ways simply because those worldly ways appear to have more substance than the kingdom. After all, if Dad says he is a Christian but his life is no different from the non-Christian, why bother with Christianity? You see, a man will rule in his home no matter what he does (and no matter what the champions of egalitarianism might say). He may rule with his wimpy example and push his wife toward an acceptance of godless feminism and his children toward Satan's counterfeit kingdom, or he can be the servant leader that Jesus Christ is for the church and lead his wife and children into sincere, effective kingdom living. In either case, the duty of leadership is "fulfilled." In other words, a Christian man will either add to the problem of a high divorce rate, effeminate men, frustrated women and self-centered, self-seeking isolated individuals or he will produce a quiver full of warriors for Christ's victorious kingdom.

### *Church Crisis*

There is a long history of a feminizing influence in the church. I will not take the time to recount the examples now. Instead, let us focus on what has happened in the North American church in the last

*The Crisis Of Our Time*

few generations.

Without the leadership of manly Christian men, the church has become a refuge for women and sissified men. All too often clergymen are soft, limp wristed types who are comfortable "ministering" to women and children yet out-of-place among men.

One of the primary reasons for the wimpish church today is an unbiblical eschatology. After all, most men don't want to be on the losing side and an eschatology that teaches a failure of the gospel until Christ's personal, physical intervention is defeatist. If you are in a fistfight and your opponent is beating the tar out of you, any objective observer will declare you the loser even if you are eventually rescued by a 6 foot 6, 300 pound, World Wrestling Federation type. That's defeat. That's being a loser. And the "any moment rapture out of this mess" mentality is a loser's mentality. It says the gospel of Jesus Christ is weak and beggarly and will not accomplish what God wants it to accomplish.

You see, there are only two views when it comes eschatology. Either you think the gospel of Jesus Christ will triumph or you believe the gospel of Jesus Christ will go down to an ignominious defeat. Don't kid yourself: there are no other choices when it comes to eschatology. The only *biblical* choice is to accept the doctrine of a victorious gospel. I accept the biblical view that the gospel of Jesus Christ *will* triumph in history. I also believe it will take many generations for victory to be realized. One of the reasons it will take such a long time (speaking humanly) is be-cause the church today is impotent and the corrective process will not take place overnight (see Leon J. Podles, *The Church Impotent: The Feminization of Christianity*).

*Men Of Issachar*

Modern North American Christians have confused the individual with the institution. The church at large has told men they are individually brides of Jesus Christ. That is not true. The truth is, each individual Christian is a *warrior* in the Army of God. Corporately we are the Body and the Bride of Jesus Christ. The institution of the church and the individual Christian are reckoned differently in the kingdom and have a very different responsibilities.

The only reason this happened is because Christian men have failed to lead in the church. They allowed pushy women and their effeminate allies in the ranks of the clergy to define the church and the role of the individual. Thus we have "God as girlfriend" theology leading to Christianity with a decidedly adolescent or feminine quality.

### *Community Crisis*

There are a number of Christian men involved in community activity but most of them are not participating as self-conscious representatives of Christ and his kingdom. Most Christian men have never taken the time to study the Bible and discern how the principles found in Scripture are applied to the civic realm. It is most important for Christian men to study the Bible so they can learn how the principles of God's law are applied in modern North American society. Indeed, even that statement is anathema to most Christians. Most church goers will recoil at the thought of making the Bible the standard of right and wrong in the community. Is it any wonder we live in a society under the rule of the devotees of power religion? Our civil government continues to accumulate power unto itself and our God-given freedoms are further eroded each day. Many people who call themselves Christians are

*The Crisis Of Our Time*

happy to see the central power become the acknowledged god of society. Meanwhile, "conservative Christians" rummage through the existing political alternatives hoping to find something that will stem the tide of the godless state but they refuse to consider the possibility that the best law for any society is God's law. Thus, we continue down the path of totalitarianism with most Christian men hoping for the "any moment rapture" so they won't have to deal with the problem.

The Bible teaches something very different. The Bible says the civil authority is a servant of Almighty God. And as a servant of Almighty God the civil authority is required to govern in a fashion pleasing to the Creator of the universe. This does not mean we are to impose Mosaic law on modern society. It means instead we are supposed to know what the Bible says about law and how the principles of God's Word are applied in this modern setting.

### *True Solutions*

The answer to all of society's ills is the gospel of Jesus Christ. The gospel of Jesus Christ tells us that mankind is sinful and in need of a Savior. The gospel of Jesus Christ tells us the only Savior available to mankind is the Eternal Son. The gospel demands submission on the part of every person. It requires people to repent and accept the substitutionary death of Jesus Christ as a means of satisfying the justice of the heavenly Father. But it does not stop there. The gospel of Jesus Christ includes instructions on how to live life as a "saved one." It says the people of God will be blessed when they live in obedience to his word. It says families will be at peace and be productive when they are ordered according to the biblical mandate. The gospel teaches that men must lead in their household in order for that household to be blessed.

Moreover, the gospel of Jesus Christ insists men are supposed to lead in the church. If they do not then the church will go astray and the blessings God has prepared for the Bride will be reserved for another generation. In addition, the gospel of Jesus Christ includes directives for the proper ordering of civic society. We are told that Jesus Christ is the Savior of all men but especially those who believe. This is to say the gospel – the good news of Christ as savior and King – will impact all of society but only when the people of God are doing what the gospel calls them to do. And the primary thing missing in the expression of the gospel today is manly leadership in the family, church and community.

The family is the basic building block of the rest of society. It is in the family that human beings learn what it means to be truly human. It is in the context of the family that boys and girls develop into men and women and it is in that first "schoolhouse" they learn about the paramount importance of the kingdom of God - or they learn to ignore it. Although it is unfashionable today to talk about male headship the fact remains that the family will not function as God intended unless men lead. The leadership men are required to furnish for the family is Christlike servant leadership. Failure to do so means the product that emerges from the factory of the family will be defective. Thus, our society is flooded with "merchandise" in desperate need of recall. Nonetheless, once the human product has left the factory it is beyond repair except by supernatural means.

Unless men do their job there is no hope for change in society. I am not suggesting God's hands

*The Crisis Of Our Time*

are tied; I am simply saying it is through the family - families led by godly men - that God has chosen to bring his kingdom to fruition on this earth.

The crisis we face today is not unique. There have been times throughout history when men of God have failed in their responsibility to lead. Eli the priest failed to lead his household and raised sons who despised the things of God. These were men who were functioning as priests in Israel and yet they cared nothing for God's law. Although they had been raised by a "man of the cloth" they considered the ministry nothing more than an easy living. They despised the sacrifices of God and made themselves fat from those things which had been dedicated to Yahweh. They satisfied their baser desires with the women who served at the door of the tabernacle. We can imagine that the circumstance in the home and family of Eli was symptomatic of a widespread problem in the whole nation of Israel.

God addressed this crisis of leadership by raising up a prophet, Samuel, the son of Elkanah and Hannah. However, even Samuel was not up to the task. Yes, he did properly discharge his duty as prophet, but like his mentor Eli, Samuel failed to lead his family in the path of righteousness. Like Eli, Samuel's sons were corrupt and their sinful character was one of the reasons (or excuses if you will) the children of Israel referenced when they asked for a king.

The king who was placed on the throne at the request of the people likewise failed as a leader in his own household. Although his sons were not corrupt like the sons of Eli or Samuel, king Saul failed to provide an example of godly manhood to his offspring and the people of Israel. He eventually lost his life in battle with the Philistines just as Samuel had said in the unusual circumstance that took place at the house of the witch of Endor (1 Samuel 28).

This crisis of leadership has been evidenced at other times in history as well.  For instance, undisciplined youth was behind the moral decay that blighted this nation at its inception (see, Daniel Dorchester, *Christianity In The United States*).  The first modern youth movement swept Europe at the beginning of the 20th century and led directly to the war to end all wars, World War One (see, Paul Johnson, *Modern Times*)

There will be those who refuse to acknowledge the reason for the problems we face today and many who will ignore this call to faithfulness.  Many men will deny their duty to lead in their own household and those who humble themselves and submit to this responsibility may be few.  As much as we may want the majority of Christian men to respond to this call, we know God often works through the few rather than the many.  Thus, those who respond to this call to lead must be prepared for the long haul.  Christian men must understand they are laying the groundwork for the next generation.  It is critical for us to lead our families in the way of the kingdom so our sons might do the same in their families.  In other words, we cannot have a short-term view.  We cannot give up the fight if we don't see dramatic change in our lifetime.  We should expect to see changes in our own households but it will take time to achieve the critical mass necessary to see wholesale change in society.

### *True Resources*

It is important to recognize that the family is central to God's purpose on earth.  The family is the basic building block of society. Without the institution of the family there is no proper church or state.

God began his work in this time space-creation with a family. If he had wanted to begin with a full-blown ecclesiastical structure or a civil society he could have created dozens, hundreds or even thousands of human beings all at once. However, God chose to create a single family, Adam and Eve, from whom would come all of mankind.

Moreover, all the requirements for leadership in the church and the civil community are nurtured within the family. The Bible tells us that unless a man can lead in his own household he is not qualified to lead in the church (1 Timothy 3:1-13, Titus 1:5-9). In Old Testament history, we find men who led in their family were able to lead others in society (Genesis 18:19). The Bible also tells us that a properly ordered family is a source of blessings for human society. For instance, the apostle Paul says children should obey and honor their parents so that their days may be long on the earth (Ephesians 6:1-3). This is the most fundamental blessing given to the people of God. Length of days enhances all else that God would do with his people in this physical realm. Again, the family is the central institution for the realization of God's kingdom.

The world says that any group of people living under the same roof should be considered family. According to the popular view, marriage between one man and one woman is not essential to the familial experience. Indeed, there is pressure in our modern society to eliminate traditional marriage so the way is opened for alternative definitions of family.

Nonetheless, the Bible presents us with God's definition of family as one man and one woman joined in the covenant of marriage. In addition, God intends that man and wife should be fruitful and multiply. Therefore, as God so blesses, family is further defined as a man, his wife and their offspring.

This does not rule out the idea of extended family. The Bible also tells us it is proper for a husband and wife to care for their close relatives who are in need. Sometimes this means members of the extended family will live in the same household. However, even in those circumstances the man of the house is supposed to lead.

The kingdom of God is realized on earth through the ministry of the family rather than the work of the church or state. The church, for instance, is not supposed to govern the activity of every individual. The civil government is not given leave by God to dictate the day to day activities of individuals and families either. Instead, the family is the incubator for the kingdom because it is there that God's ways are taught to the next generation. It is within the context of family that the work of bringing creation under the dominion of Almighty God takes place. This might be through a family business but is often as mundane as a head of the household guiding the development of his family as he works to support them punching a clock at the local factory. In any case, it is within the arena of the family that the rubber meets the road. Families bring the authority of Jesus Christ to bear on this creation by walking in obedience to his law. Heads of households are given the responsibility to teach their spouse and children the ways of God and to model Christlikeness so they have a proper example to imitate.

As the head of the household brings his sphere of influence under the authority of Jesus

## *The Crisis Of Our Time*

Christ, he not only provides a model worthy of imitation but he brings the reign of the Messiah to bear on everything for which he is responsible. The way he works his job should be an example of how to do everything as unto the Lord. The manner in which he treats his wife should be a reflection of Christ's relationship to his Bride the church. How he spends his free time should be worthy of imitation by his children and others that he comes in contact with as he works out his salvation with fear and trembling (Philippians 2:12-13). A man must work, relax, vote, learn, lead and do everything as unto the Lord. When this is done on a consistent basis, his arena of responsibility will exhibit the results of a life lived in obedience to the King of Kings. As more and more Christian men do so, the different spheres of influence represented by each man will overlap and Christ's Lordship will be revealed in this realm across a broad spectrum.

Some may say the church is the primary institution in God's kingdom. This is true in a sense; only the church lasts into eternity. Christ said that in eternity mankind is not married nor given in marriage. The Bride of Christ, however, is eternal. Yet, the Bride cannot function properly in this realm unless men of Christ are fulfilling their responsibilities as leaders. So, in that sense, the family is the primary institution. It is fundamental to the health of the church and civil society.

Additionally, the banding together of families creates the local expression of the body of Jesus Christ. This is not to say a gathering of families can ignore proper ecclesiastical structure. Instead, it simply recognizes that churches are made up of several families coming together for worship.

*Men Of Issachar*

Both family and church mirror Trinity in its community and leadership paradigm. Indeed, the Bible tells us we are designed for community, a place where iron sharpens iron and so we cannot neglect the fellowship of the believers. In coming together as members of Christ's body, Christian men are able to find mentors to help them in the work of leadership. Additionally, as Christian families join together in fellowship, urging one another on to greater godliness, they will be examples to society at large - a city set on a hill - a gathering of people that cannot be ignored.

It is also within this fellowship of Believers that Christian men are held accountable for their obligation before God. No man of Christ should attempt to fulfill his duties of leadership alone. This is not to say someone else can step in and do what he should do; it simply means all of us must be accountable to someone else for our behavior. Thus, Paul says we are to submit one to another and we are to encourage each other on to greater godliness. This is especially important for men of Christ. The world is constantly trying to discourage men from fulfilling their duty of leadership. Like a three strand cord, men held accountable by other heads of households and properly established church leadership, find their task of headship easier to bear.

Men of Christ have the responsibility to lead their own families but they also have the responsibility to lead in the church and civil community. Indeed, proven leadership in the home *qualifies* a man for church and civil leadership. This does not mean every man will become a church leader or a civil legislator. However, every church or civic authority should *first* be an effective leader at home.

With all this talk about men as leaders it may seem that I am diminishing the role of mothers. That is not my intention. This book is about the duty of men and so I will naturally focus my attention on that subject. However, I should mention that a good leader will always make use of his human resources. Every man of Christ must care for his wife and children so they can fulfill their duties before the Lord as well as he does. The Bible is clear in stating that mothers have a responsibility to teach children in the home. Women of Christ must strive to be good examples to others in the household just as men of God should. Mothers have the responsibility to submit to their husbands but this does not mean they are expected to be nonentities in the home. As we will see in a later chapter, a man of Christ is only effective as a leader when he is in right relationship with his wife.

Children have a responsibility in the Christian home as well. Children are commanded to obey their parents. They are to honor them and to learn from them. Children do not have the option of ignoring the instruction of their father and mother but will be held accountable before God for disobedience and rebellion.

I do not believe I am overstating the case when I say the future of this nation rests on the shoulders of Christian men. God's will shall be done; if this generation fails to walk in obedience before him he will raise up another. God will find a generation that is truly committed to the kingdom.

## *True Commitment*

The Bible tells us blessings come through obedience. We are not blessed by God as a natural

*Men Of Issachar*

consequence of living in the United States of America. Instead, the Bible clearly says God blesses his people when they obey his law. These blessings are typically bestowed upon people as a corporate entity more than isolated individuals. In other words, when many households are laboring to bring their arena of activity under the Lordship of Jesus Christ, the covenant blessings are realized on earth.

What about the fact that we are not under law but under grace? If we are not under the law how can we expect to be blessed for obedience to God's law? Well, to say we are not under the law is to say we are no longer in the natural state. The Bible does not tell us we can ignore God's law once we are born again. In fact, Paul says that through faith we fulfill the law.

It is important to understand the changes that have taken place in the law with the fulfillment of God's intention in Jesus Christ. Jesus said that not even the smallest stroke of a pen would change in the law until heaven and earth passed away (Matthew 5:18). At the same time, the writer of the book of Hebrews tells us that with the change of the priesthood there is by necessity a change in the law (Hebrews 7:12). It seems these two statements are in contradiction. But that is because we do not understand the style of language Jesus was using when he said he had come to fulfill the law and that nothing would change in the law until heaven and earth had passed away. Jesus meant nothing would change in the law until the new covenant was inaugurated and the old covenant was passing away. Indeed,

> A person at all familiar with the phraseology of the Old Testament scriptures, knows that the

dissolution of the Mosaic economy, and the establishment of the Christian, is often spoken of as the removing of the old earth and heavens, and the creation of a new earth and new heavens. For example, "For behold, I create new heavens and a new earth: and the former shall not be remembered, nor come into mind." "For as the new heavens and the new earth which I will make shall remain before me, saith the Lord, so shall your seed and your name remain." The period of the close of the one dispensation, and the commencement of the other, is spoken of as "the last days," and "the end of the world;" and is described as such a shaking of the earth and heavens, as should lead to the removal of the things which were shaken (see, John Brown, *Sayings and Discourses Of Christ, vol. 1)*

In other words, Jesus was saying nothing would change until the new covenant came into being and the old covenant began to close (Hebrews 8:13). This does not mean we can throw out old testament law. Instead, it means the law is no longer an external goad but is part of the new creation, having been written upon our heart (Jeremiah 31:31-34, Hebrews 8:7-12). It means we have the responsibility to cultivate the internalized law as an expression of Christlikeness. Jesus Christ fulfilled the law and the prophets and we are supposed to imitate him by fulfilling them as well. Our fulfillment is analogical and focused on being an example of Christ to the world. And Christlikeness has been objectively defined for us in the pages of Scripture. We are not supposed to do whatever "feels right" but are commanded to walk even as Jesus walked (1 John 2:6). Certainly we no longer participate in the Mosaic ritual but it is just as certain that we have the responsibility to obey the law of God as it has been fulfilled, clarified and applied in Jesus Christ.

This means we can claim all the covenant promises of God in Jesus Christ (2 Corinthians 1:20). It means, in Christ, we are heirs to the covenant expectations of Abraham. It also means we are responsible for keeping the stipulations of the covenant; we have been grafted into Israel and so we partake of Israel's responsibilities. This must be understood as presented to us in the New Testament fulfillment and application of God's law. This is not the place for a thorough study of how to apply God's law in this New Testament age. Suffice it to say the modern church has been lax in her obedience to God's Word. Too often we substitute legal-ism for obedience and decry any attempt to apply God's law in this life and realm. The law primarily reveals the character of God to us and therefore assists us in thinking as he thinks. For instance, murder is wrong because it is contrary to God's character not because it is "not nice" or contrary to "natural law." We must study the Bible in order to learn what it means to fulfill the law in faith.

Thus it is critical for men of Christ to know the Bible. Every man must be a student of Scripture and a warrior in prayer. Every man of Christ must make it his ambition to be a practical theologian, especially in his particular area of expertise. In other words, every man should seek to know how God's Word applies to his specific sphere of influence. If he is a business owner he needs to know how to apply God's Word to that peculiar activity. If he is a legislator he needs to understand he is a minister of the most high God and so has a responsibility to apply God's law (as understood in this New Testament age) to his arena of responsibility. The examples are numerous but the point is simply this;

*The Crisis Of Our Time*

every man of Christ must study the Word and know how to apply it in every situation he may meet with.

Some men may feel they do not have time for constant study of God's Word. Yet, I suspect these same men find time for watching TV or other trivial activities. Really it is a matter of priorities. The man whose treasure is in heaven will certainly make room for the study of God's Word so he can understand how to fulfill his duty as a husband, father, employee or employer and so on.

There is no guarantee that the man who fulfills his responsibility is going to meet with success as defined by his friends and relatives. The Bible tells us that after certain deeds of faithfulness which King Hezekiah performed, Sennacherib, king of Syria, came and besieged Jerusalem (2 Chronicles 32:1). One would think that after deeds of faithfulness a man could expect blessings from the hand of God. Generally that is the case. Yet, God is sovereign and he will do as he sees fit. Another example is Job, a godly man who nonetheless found himself in the midst of terrible hardship. Both Job and Hezekiah were primary players in the spiritual battle raging in the heavenly realm. In fact, we might say they *were* blessed for their righteous behavior because they were chosen by God to participate in a cosmic contest. Hezekiah, he participated in the supernatural destruction of the Assyrian army without raising a hand in anger. Job had the reputation of Yahweh riding on his commitment to the Almighty and because of his faithfulness, played a primary part in the humiliation of the accuser.

You must be willing to do whatever God calls you to do. You may anticipate blessings for obedience yet you cannot demand that God's grace conform to your expectation. Your duty is to obey with joy and leave the final outcome to the Lord.

# CHAPTER 2
## MEN OF ISSACHAR

*Of Issachar, men who had understanding of the times, to know what Israel ought to do, 200 chiefs, and all their kinsmen under their command* (1 Chronicles 12:32, English Standard Version)

There was a time in the history of Israel when all was in turmoil. The leadership of the land had taken the kingdom down a wicked path and it seemed there was no turning back. It was as if the nation had become a hollow shell, ready to implode. In addition, the long-time ruler of the nation died in battle and the resulting leadership vacuum quickly led to civil war. Those were desperate times. The future of the nation hung in the balance. It was a time that required bold leadership. It was a time suited for the chief men of Issachar, who understood the times and knew what Israel ought to do.

In first Chronicles chapter twelve, we read about the various groups of armed men from the twelve tribes of Israel who gathered in Hebron to make David king. David had ruled Judah from Hebron for at least two years while civil war raged between Judah and the tribes that followed the house

*Men Of Issachar*

of Saul. Two events changed this circumstance: the death of Abner, the commander of Israel's army and the death of Ishbosheth, Saul's son who ruled from east of the Jordan in the city of Mahanaim. In both cases David was innocent. Abner had been murdered by Joab, the commanding general of David's army. Joab did this to avenge the death of his brother Asahel (2 Samuel 2:17-23). Later, Ishbosheth was killed by two men while he rested in his private room. In both situations, David promptly separated himself from the perpetrators; the men who killed Ishbosheth were executed and Joab was cursed by David. It is important for us to realize that David was innocent of the deaths of these two men and so could not be accused of seeking the throne through intrigue.

Once the way had been made clear for the fulfillment of God's promise concerning David's rule, the tribes came to Hebron in order to make him king over all Israel. In the roll-call recorded in first Chronicles twelve, we see that most tribes sent a large contingent of warriors to represent them. However, in the case of Issachar, just 200 men came to Hebron. Unlike the other tribes, Issachar did not send a force of rank and file fighting men but sent the princes to represent the entire tribe.

This show of strength on the part of the tribes (including Issachar) was designed to forestall any rebellion against the decision to make David king. Up until this time Israel had been in constant turmoil. From the time that Saul became King and David rose to prominence, Saul spent most of his time in pursuit of Jesse's son, hoping to destroy him and make his own dynasty secure. However, this was not God's plan. Eventually the house of Saul was nearly wiped out, opening the door for David to become king. Although representatives from all the tribes arrived in Hebron to make David King after the house of Saul was defeated, our focus in this chapter will be on the men of Issachar who understood the times and knew what Israel ought to do. Our text for this chapter is 1 Chronicles 12:32 and reads, *Of Issachar, men who had understanding of the times, to know what Israel ought to do, 200 chiefs, and all their kinsmen under their command* (English Standard Version). Who were these men of Issachar? When we ask that question we are not limited to the 200 leaders who came to Hebron.

### *Issachar*

One way to understand the character of the tribe of Issachar is to begin with the prophecy concerning the clan as delivered by Jacob, Israel himself. In Genesis 49:14 we read, *Issachar is a strong donkey, crouching between the sheepfolds. He saw that a resting place was good, and that the land was pleasant, so he bowed his shoulder to bear, and became a servant at forced labor.*

The prophecies Jacob delivered concerning his sons (and the tribes that would come from them) tell us about the character of the men, their families and clans. For instance, Jacob prophesied concerning the eventual ascendancy of Judah. He said the scepter would not depart from between Judah's feet until Shiloh came. This of course concerned Judah's royal destiny in the house of David and the coming of the Messiah, the offspring of Judah and David.

Therefore we can rest assured the character of each tribe is accurately presented by Jacob in his prophecy. When we are told Issachar is a "strong donkey lying down between two burdens" we get a

*Men Of Issachar*

picture of a "robust race, with a pleasant inheritance inviting to ease, as not requiring such toil as less fertile lands; ease at the cost of liberty" (Fausset's *Bible Dictionary*). In short, we see a tribe noted for strength, laziness and frequent complacency (cf. Deuteronomy 33:18-19).

It is interesting that one of the ways a strong, robust people might get ahead in the world is by hiring themselves out for occasional "dirty work." By this I refer to the tendency of some people groups to engage in mercenary warfare. When a tribe or a clan hires itself out as mercenary soldiers they do so for money without too many strings attached. Obviously there is risk of injury or death but there is very little responsibility. It is a quick and "easy" way to earn money without the burden of patriotic duty. It seems at least one clan in Issachar may have resorted to mercenary activity as a means of gaining wealth and influence. In 1 Chronicles 7:1-5 we read a census of the tribe possibly near the end of David's reign: *The sons of Issachar: Tola, Puah, Jashub, and Shimron, four. The sons of Tola: Uzzi, Rephaiah, Jeriel, Jahmai, Ibsam, and Shemuel, heads of their fathers' houses, namely of Tola, mighty warriors of their generations, their number in the days of David being 22,600. The son of Uzzi: Izrahiah. And the sons of Izrahiah: Michael, Obadiah, Joel, and Isshiah, all five of them were chief men. And along with them, by their generations, according to their fathers' houses, were units of the army for war, 36,000, for they had many wives and sons. Their kinsmen belonging to all the clans of Issachar were in all 87,000 mighty warriors, enrolled by genealogy.*

According to the text, there was a clan within

*Men Of Issachar*

Issachar that was able to muster 36,000 troops ready for war ("for they had many wives and sons"), and another that could gather 22,600 mighty warriors in the days of David. The entire tribe could muster 87,000 men but these two clans are mentioned apart from the total number of able-bodied fighting men in the tribe. This may be because they were men for hire. In 1 Chronicles 7:1-5, "no less than 36,000 of its men were marauding mercenary 'bands (*giduwdim*) of soldiers for war,' a term applied elsewhere only to Gad's 'troops' and to the irregular bodies of Bedouin-like tribes round Israel (Fausset's *Bible Dictionary*). It appears they are placed into these two separate groups (as were other tribal clans) because each clan had their own "business" in the trade of warfare.

In any case, the tribe of Issachar was able to muster a large fighting force and yet we know from the history of Israel that Issachar had been allotted a relatively small portion of the Promised Land. Moreover, it was a part of the land controlled by the Canaanites for a long while. The allotment of Issachar was in the region known (in a time of Jesus) as Galilee. It was an agriculturally rich region that would have allowed the tribe of Issachar to live well without ridding the land of the original inhabitants – or indeed without much effort at all.

If we put all this together, we get a picture of a tribe that has the ability to wage war and is blessed with rich natural resources yet wastes its potential. They were a blessed tribe - blessed with strength, courage and a rich land but cursed with laziness and complacency. Because they preferred to take the easy way out, they bowed their shoulder to bear a burden and became a band of slaves, failing to rid their inheritance of the Canaanite tribes.

This is not to say the tribe of Issachar was wholly without ambition. In the days of the judges, Tola arose from the tribe of Issachar and judged Israel for 23 years (Judges 10:1-2). Moreover in the days of the divided monarchy there were two kings who came from the house of Issachar. Baasha, used by God to fulfill the prophecy against the house of Jeroboam and the son of Baasha, named Elah. Baasha reigned for 24 years and his son for two. The action of Baasha against the house of Jeroboam reminds us of the war-like character of the tribe.

### Men Of Issachar

Now, in the days when Israel gathered in Hebron to make David king, Issachar was represented by 200 leading men. They were chiefs who arrived in Hebron to declare the will of the entire tribe. Are we to assume this was simply a cultural phenomenon? In other words was the tribe of Issachar represented by men simply because that was the way things were in the ancient near Eastern culture of Israel? I suppose we could say yes and no. Yes, because that was the norm, but no, because it was not simply a cultural phenomenon. God had determined from the beginning of time that men should lead (see Werner Neuer, *Man and Woman In Christian Perspective*) In other words God created man to lead at home, in the church and community. Anytime we say something like this it is typical to immediately qualify the statement and point out that God will sometimes raise a woman to a position of leadership. I'll follow the trend just so no one can call me a chauvinist. For example, in the days of the judges, Deborah judged Israel and was the leader who sent Barak into battle (incidentally, the tribe of

Issachar participated in that campaign against the Canaanites). Other examples include Huldah, the prophetess who pronounced judgment against Judah because of the sins of Manassah and Priscilla, the wife of Aquila, who, in concert with her husband, took Apollos aside and explained to him the way of God more accurately. However, my goal is not to provide a catalog of the exceptions to the rule. My focus is on the fact that God created men to lead.

Adam was created first and given the task of working the garden and exercising dominion over all the earth. Indeed he was taken from the earth that he might "return" to the earth as one who has authority over creation under God. Later, God created Eve from a portion of Adam's body, scooped out from the side of the man (the Bible indicates God used more than just a rib). The Scripture tells us she was presented to Adam as his helpmeet. Certainly she had a role in the task of dominion just as women do today. Nevertheless, Adam was created first and man is supposed to be the leader in his own home, in the church and indeed in society at large (1 Timothy 2:12-15).

Therefore, it is not simply a reflection of the culture of the day that we see recorded in 1 Chronicles 12:32. The men of Issachar arrived in Hebron to throw their weight behind David's kingship because it is *men* who are given the primary task of leadership. This is especially evident when leadership involves risk to life and limb and when visionary thinking is required.

This is not to say that women are called to submit to men in general. That has never been the case. A wife is supposed to submit to one man and that one man is her husband (see, R. J. Rushdoony,

*Men Of Issachar*

*The Institutes Of Biblical Law).* The only way she might legitimately submit to a man other than her husband is when she is submitted to lawful ecclesiastical or civil leadership, just like any other man or woman might be. In other words, a man is the head of his own household but he also submits to leadership in the church or in the workplace or in the civil realm. This is true for the woman as well. She is in submission to her husband but she is also in submission to legitimate authority in the church, workplace or civil realm. Thus, men and women alike are duty-bound to submit to God-ordained authority in a variety of spheres.

And so the chiefs of Issachar came as civil and military leaders representing the tribe. They came to Hebron to proclaim the readiness of their tribe to go to war in order to secure the throne for David. This is really what it was about. It was a show of force by the tribes of Israel to say to those who may not be inclined to accept David as king that they were ready and willing to take up arms on behalf of the son of Jesse.

The other tribes sent military units of fighting men while Issachar sent only their chiefs. The chiefs were able to say with confidence that the entire tribe - all 87,000 fighting men - would heed the call to duty on behalf of David. Those 87,000 were submitted to the leadership of the 200. The 200 leaders both represented the temper of the tribe and, as leaders, helped mold it. True, the tribe of Issachar was a warlike people but it required the leadership of the 200 men to ensure movement in a godly, productive direction.

## Understood The Times

We are also told the chief men of Issachar

understood the times. For instance, they understood that the situation in Israel was volatile. There was a leadership vacuum with the death of Abner and Ishbosheth and because of this void anything might have happened. The subsequent history of Israel bears this out. At times there would be a rapid succession of kings in Israel much like a modern Third World country, constantly roiled by coups and general unrest.

Additionally, Israel and Judah had enemies on every side. In fact, at the time these events were taking place, the Philistines had pushed far inland, severing Israel and Judah into separate parts. This is the reason Ishbosheth had his capital on the east side of the Jordan at the royal city of Mahanaim (The name means "double camp" and commemorates the experience of Jacob when he was returning to the land of promise and met the angel of God just prior to his encounter with Esau). Ishbosheth fled his Father's capital of Gibeah as the Philistines took advantage of the turmoil surrounding the death of Saul, advancing deep into Israelite territory.

The men of Issachar also understood David was the best man for the job based upon his experience as a captain of the armies of Israel. He had proven himself while he served Saul and as the leader of the outcast band in Ziklag. In addition, David had shown his mettle under more "civilized conditions" by ruling Judah from Hebron for at least two years.

Moreover, the men of Issachar understood the promises of the patriarchs were to be fulfilled in David's line. I believe their understanding was much more than the ability to read the temper of the times. They truly understood the times because they recog-

*Men Of Issachar*

nized David's anointing as proof of God's intention to confirm his covenant with Israel in the house of David. They knew Saul and his house had been rejected by God. They knew the son of Jesse was the one through whom God was going to bless Israel.

Therefore, the men of Issachar were not merely following the crowd. They did give energy to an existing movement but they were not the kind of men who would lift a dampened finger to the breeze in order to choose a course of action.

A Jewish paraphrase of this Scripture suggests the men of Issachar knew the times in that they understood the astrological signs which pointed to seasons, years and special events in God's government of creation (Genesis 1:14). If that was the case, perhaps they were able to read the astral phenomenon pertaining to David's ascension to the throne of Israel. We cannot determine this beyond a doubt from this short passage of Scripture but there is reason to believe the Jewish comments on this passage are accurate. We know the heavenly realm was created to help guide mankind in their quest for the Messiah. This is exemplified in the actions of the Magi who came to Israel from a far country because the heavens told them the Messiah was born. Since the heavens actively proclaimed the intent and purpose of God up until the completion of his plans in Jesus, we cannot discount the possibility the men of Issachar had understanding of the times as it concerned the voice of the heavens. Perhaps there was some sort of astral phenomenon that proclaimed David as crucial to the messianic line.

These were men of understanding in a godly sense as well. They did not approach the problems of civil leadership with unaided human reason. Instead

*Men Of Issachar*

they drew upon the wisdom of God. Indeed, it is only when one is guided by "God think" they can be described as "understanding."

Extra-biblical Jewish works say the men of Issachar were the wisest men in the Sanhedrin. This means they would be men who sought, *to know wisdom and instruction, to understand words of insight, to receive instruction in wise dealing, in righteousness, justice, and equity; to give prudence to the simple, knowledge and discretion to the youth - Let the wise hear and increase in learning, and the one who understands obtain guidance, to understand a proverb and a saying, the words of the wise and their riddles. The fear of the LORD is the beginning of knowledge; fools despise wisdom and instruction* (Proverbs 1:2-7). In any case, we can rest assured the men of Issachar were well schooled in God's wisdom. They knew the law and they knew how to apply it. They recognized the sound wisdom of David and embraced him as king. As those who were godly in their thinking they remained loyal to God's anointed until God himself removed Saul and his house from leadership. Once events began to fulfill God's previously ordained plan, they're ready to act accordingly.

Therefore we conclude they were skilled statesmen who understood the times and understood how to direct the will of the people so their tribe might walk in the path of wisdom. They understood how to appeal to the tribe of Issachar because they were men of the people and not of the ivory tower. Their understanding was honored by the tribe of Issachar and they had full confidence in their chiefs.

In a nutshell, the leaders of Issachar understood the times in view of the past, the present and the future. They had seen how God had dealt with Israel in the past and how he had dealt with the house of Saul. They recognized the danger Israel was in and viewed the vacuum of leadership with concern. They recognized David was a man God had called to leadership and they saw that the future of Israel was tied to the future of the house of David. Truly these were men of understanding.

### *Knew What Israel Should Do*

These leaders of Issachar knew what their own tribe should do and what the entire nation of Israel should do. The application of their understanding was not limited to their separate clans or tribe but to the people of God as a whole. The chiefs of Issachar realized what was good for one tribe was good for all and they knew God's wisdom is never limited to a certain class of people. In other words, because God rules over all of creation, all of creation must submit to his wisdom.

Furthermore, their knowledge of what Israel should do was not based on pragmatic concerns. In other words, they were not supporting the house of David merely to avoid inter-tribal warfare. They supported David because it was a godly course of action.

Up until this point there were some in Israel who thought the house of Saul should continue to rule. There were others who had been hoping, for years, that David would seize the throne. But the men of Issachar realized Israel should do this because it was what God wanted. God's will for David was well known. Samuel the Prophet had anointed David as king a dozen years previously and the men of Issachar knew the time had come for all Israel to acknowledge that.

## Men Of Issachar

It was not enough for the people of Israel to simply talk about David becoming king. Something had to be done. Action had to be taken. And so the gathering of the tribes had to be more than a simple conference to set up a committee to study the problem. The men of Issachar were men of action.

This brings up another difference between the leadership of men and the leadership of women. For the most part, men are proactive in leadership. They want to get something done and get it done quickly. Now, sometimes it is best to go slowly but in the world of politics it is usually best to move quickly and decisively. This is especially true when civil government remains within its proper bounds. In other words, bold, decisive action in politics is a virtue when civil government is limited to is appropriate role. The primary duties of civil government are to bring unity and security while protecting the citizens from foreign and domestic aggression. When civil government moves beyond its proper function we see a "need" for a slow and deliberate process of government. In other words, the "nanny state" governs much like a woman manages her household. A woman managing her household will not do a very good job if she is quick to make decisions and acts with boldness and force. On the other hand, a state limited to its proper duty must act with alacrity and force because its work is not to provide healthcare for everyone (for instance) but to apprehend and punish evildoers within the borders of the nation and those who would attack from the outside.

The men of Issachar knew what Israel should do. They knew Israel was supposed to take action to install David as king rather than hem and haw. The opportunity to establish the throne of David was upon them and it was time to act. The men of Issachar were so certain of this, they were willing to fight for what was right and they knew that all Israel should do the same if necessary.

## *Still Like Issachar*

Christian men of this age are all too often like Issachar of old. We have a heritage of courage in the face of difficulty, but living in the land of plenty has made many of us inclined to take the easy way out when faced with hardship. We find it easy to compromise with the "Canaanites." We would rather rest beneath life's burdens until we encounter a challenge that promises personal gain.

Christian men still have the ability to wage war on behalf of king Jesus but it is easier to leave the fighting to somebody else – all too often to our wives. Christian men have been blessed with abundant spiritual resources and in this country, material resources as well. Yet, we often lack the commitment required to fulfill our leadership duty and achieve our full potential in Christ. We are blessed men - blessed with Christ's strength and courage and a rich inheritance in his kingdom. Like ancient Issachar, we forfeit what could be ours due to our laziness and complacency. Refusing to lead in the way we ought, we bow our shoulders to bear a burden and become a band of slaves, failing to take possession of our covenant inheritance.

## *Nevertheless, Men Still Lead*

God's design for leadership is the same today as it was in the days of David's enthronement over Israel and as it was on the day he created Adam. Much of the resistance to this design stems from the fact that men have not exercised leadership in a godly fashion for generations. Christian men are

*Men Of Issachar*

more like the bands of Issachar than the chiefs. We are at ease in a land of plenty, mercenaries for whom work is the end rather than the means. We are content to be a band of slaves (to our own appetites, our job, our society and so on), as long as our personal peace and comfort are not too badly disrupted. After all, pursuing a life of Christlike leadership would disrupt the status-quo and *certainly* lead to an uncomfortable circumstance.

According to the Bible, leadership is supposed to be self-sacrificing. Whether a man is exercising leadership in his home, at church, on the job or in the civil realm, leadership must always be self-denying.

We understand what this might look like in the home setting even if we rarely see it in action. We understand that when the Bible says a man is called to love his wife "even as Christ loved the church and gave himself up for her" he is supposed to think of her more highly than himself. A man who is a proper leader in his home will have no problem with an unsubmissive wife. Problems typically arise when a man is not exercising leadership as he should. Either he refuses to lead at all or he attempts to lead in a heavy-handed fashion. This is why the whole idea of authority and submission has gotten a bad rap. Not because the concept is wrong but because those who claim to be followers of Christ have failed to lead as Jesus leads.

Therefore, when we say men are supposed to lead, we must begin with the truth that men are supposed to be servant leaders. Jesus said leadership in the kingdom is about service. He did not limit servant leadership to the home. In fact, when he told his apostles the first would be last, he said as much in the context of civic leadership. In Mark 10:42-45 we read, *And Jesus called them to him and said to them, "You know that those who are considered rulers of the Gentiles lord it over them, and their great ones exercise authority over them. But it shall not be so among you. But whoever would be great among you must be your servant, and whoever would be first among you must be slave of all. For even the Son of Man came not to be served but to serve, and to give his life as a ransom for many."*

So, Jesus talks about servant leadership in the context of the civil realm. Granted, none of his apostles were thinking about running for mayor of Jerusalem but in light of the circumstance (James and John wanting to be first and second in the kingdom of God) and the nature of Jesus' answer, we understand that *all* leadership - at any level - is supposed to be servant leadership. We used to understand this (to some degree) in this country. When we called our elected officials "public servants" it actually meant something. It doesn't anymore. Nowadays leadership is not about self-sacrifice but about self aggrandizement and power.

My point is very simply that men must still lead. Again, I'm not going to discuss those areas where women can and do exercise leadership; my focus is on the need for men to lead. And men must lead in the family, in the church and in the civil realm. They must lead as husbands and fathers in the family, they must lead as elders and deacons in the church and they must lead in the community. This is what God created man to do. This is the primary characteristic of godly manhood. It is incumbent upon you as a man of God to lead in the arena of activity you have been given.

## *Men Of Issachar*

Like the men of Issachar, Christian men may look to their heritage for inspiration. We do that when we read about our family history in the Bible. Sacred history is our history. In Christ, the heroes of the faith are part of our pedigree.

We can also look to our personal family history and from that history learn from both the good and the bad examples. In my own family I recall my grandfather on my Father's side and see a Christian man willing to give up everything to pursue the call of God. My grandfather worked at Bunker Hill silver mine in Kellogg Idaho and had been employed there for nearly 40 years. Yet, some time before his retirement he resigned and went into full-time Christian service with New Tribes Mission. He was willing to step out of his comfort zone and lead his family in the direction he believed God was leading.

My Father is another good example to Christian men. He was willing to take his family down a theologically unfamiliar path, one difficult for his family to accept. Nonetheless he shouldered the mantle of godly headship and led his family into a deeper understanding of the kingdom of God. Indeed, my father followed in his father's footsteps by committing himself to the full-time Christian ministry and ministered as a pastor for 20 years.

Christian men in this day can look to their personal heritage and to the example of Scripture to encourage them in taking up the mantle of leadership. It is not as if Christian men have an option. They will lead in one way or another. Either they will lead poorly and see their family (and church) go to seed or they will lead well and have the joy of bringing their family into a deeper understanding of

Christ and his kingdom. The same is true in the workplace and civil realm. Christian men will lead well or they will lead poorly. If they lead poorly in the workplace, they will reinforce the bad behavior of others. If they lead well, they will be a shining example of how one is supposed to bring their arena of activity under the authority of Jesus Christ. In the civil realm they will lead poorly by remaining uninformed and inactive or they will lead well through active participation in the legislative process and in understanding the times. This leads to our second point of application.

### Men Still Need To Understand The Times

Christian men need to understand the times in relationship to the past, present and future. Our examination of the times must be conducted in light of God's Word because our understanding must be based upon God's wisdom not man's. We cannot hope to understand the times with unaided human reason. It is only a sanctified intellect that can grasp the situation and make sense of it. This is why Paul says, *I appeal to you therefore, brothers, by the mercies of God, to present your bodies as a living sacrifice, holy and acceptable to God, which is your spiritual worship. Do not be conformed to this world, but be transformed by the renewal of your mind, that by testing you may discern what is the will of God, what is good and acceptable and perfect* (Romans 12:1-2).

To understand the times is to think the way God thinks and to apply our sanctified intellect to the task of making sense of this world. We need to know God's Word and know how to apply the principles of the Scripture to our current circumstance. This involves an understanding of how God has worked with his people in the past. We discern this through a study of Scripture and as we study our own history as the people of God. We also recognize this as we study more recent history – and most importantly for our purposes, the colonial history of this nation.

Furthermore, if we hope to understand the times we must know God's desire for this present age. We recognize the past is a guide but not an ironclad template. We recognize God's truth never changes but that our understanding of truth deepens and the proper application of truth will need to be adjusted as the times change. For instance, the law concerning the duty to help an enemy when his donkey collapses under its load cannot be applied in a literal fashion today even though the principal remains valid (Exodus 23:4-5). Nowadays we would obey that particular law by pulling over to help our enemy who is alongside the road with a flat tire. I suppose you could say we are obeying that law literally but I prefer to acknowledge the fact that the principle is unchanging while the application must change with the times.

Therefore we need to understand God's will for this time. We need to understand how to apply his law in this age. We need to understand how we do that in the family, church and state.

Godly understanding also seeks to know God's desire for the future. We are able to do this only in a limited sense. We do know God desires the knowledge of the Lord to cover the earth as the water covers the sea (Isaiah 11:9). The Bible tells us so. In other words, the Bible tells us the gospel will triumph in this age. The Bible is opposed to any theology suggesting the gospel of Jesus Christ is destined to fail. Hence, we know God's will for the future at least

*Men Of Issachar*

as it pertains to the success of the gospel. Because we know God desires the victory of Christ's rule, we must work to bring our sphere of influence under the lordship of Christ and lay the groundwork for future evangelism. Again, this is true in the way we lead at home, at church and in the marketplace.

So, we must be students of history, current events and cultural trends. But we must be students of the Bible first and foremost. We must be men who seek a deeper personal relationship with Jesus Christ. Only then will we be able to understand the times. This leads us to our final point in this section.

### *Men Still Need To Know What To Do*

Christian men need to know what to do personally, in their family and in the community. Christian men need to be able to look at a situation, evaluate it and come up with a God honoring course of action.

Every Christian man should look at his life with a critical eye - through the lens of God's Word as fulfilled in Jesus Christ. It isn't difficult to discern what needs to be done if one is truthful. God's Word is clear about how a Christian man should lead and about his duty to think as God thinks. Therefore, when a man's life deviates from God's standard it is evident what he should do.

Jesus said we must be willing to deal violently with the things in our life that keep us from coming under his authority. He said the kingdom of God suffers violence and violent men take it by force. He meant the kingdom of God requires violent spiritual and mental action on the part of men in order to rid themselves of the sin that keeps them from walking in obedience to Jesus Christ. For example, Christian men must labor strenuously to overcome the lack of

*Men Of Issachar*

love that is so often evident in their "leadership."

Once a Christian man has begun to put into practice the things necessary to bring his own life under the reign of Christ, he must look to his family and discover what he ought to do as a leader at home. Indeed, this would be simultaneous with putting his personal life in order.

To understand what should be done in his own household he needs to be aware of what is going on in the lives of his wife and children. He needs to be leading them in the study of Scripture and in prayer. He needs to spend time with family so he knows how they think and what they are dealing with on a day to day basis. Then, because he understands the times and understands God's Word, he can help his family in performing their duties before God. He can lead his wife and children by teaching and example. By the way, without the example the teaching will be of little use. This is something I have learned the hard way. I can say the right things, have the right theology and be doctrinally correct but if my example does not match up with what I say I will fail to lead my household in the path of righteousness.

This is true outside the home as well. Christian men must be willing to step out of their comfort zone and participate in the life of the church and community in order to express the rule of Jesus Christ to a wider audience. Thus, a Christian man should know what needs to be done in the church and civil realm. But he does more than simply acknowledge the fact something needs to be done; he actually does it. A Christian man looks at the situation in his church, evaluates the circumstance in light of the Bible and does his part to lead his church in the direction it ought to go. If he is not in a leadership position, he should work within the framework of ecclesiastical headship and lead by example. Again, the Christian man looks at the state of affairs in his community, evaluates the circumstance in light of the Bible and does his part to lead his community in the direction it ought to go (more on leadership in action in a later chapter).

Knowing what we must do as individuals, as families, as a church or community depends upon knowledge of Scripture and the leading of the Holy Spirit. It also depends upon the *experience* of putting God's Word into practice. Therefore, we will implement what we know should be done one small step at a time. As our experience grows, we will stride forward in leadership with more confidence. Not confidence in our own ability but confidence in the Lord Jesus Christ working through us. Not confidence in our wisdom but in the wisdom of God as the Holy Spirit empowers us.

## *Conclusion*

We live in troubled times and it is my conviction that nothing is going to change until the men of Issachar understand the times and know what Israel ought to do. Nothing in our society will change until Christian men embrace the wisdom of God and lead those within their sphere of influence down the path of Christlikeness. Our families, the church and our nation are in a fix because men of Christ have failed to do the job they have been called to do. Christian men have abandoned their duty as fathers, they have abandoned the church, they have abandoned their responsibility as leaders in the workplace and community. Until men of Christ fulfill their obligations nothing will change. If we continue to abdicate our responsibility, this nation will continue to slide toward absolute godlessness. I am not suggesting the gospel of Jesus Christ will go down to defeat. Instead, I am telling you that God will raise up another generation to accomplish his work.

Now is the time for the men of Issachar to arise. In these dark days it is time for Christian men to walk even as Jesus walked and to bring the authority of Christ to bear on every aspect of life.

# CHAPTER 3
## MEN OF CHRIST

*Be on the alert; stand firm in the faith; acquit yourselves like men; be strong* (1 Corinthians 16:13 Weymouth Translation)

      The Bible provides two kinds of examples to guide us in our walk as Christian men. At the very beginning of Scripture we read about Adam and so have an example of a man who did not walk in the ways of God. Indeed, throughout the whole of Scripture we find stories of men who did not walk as men of Christ. These examples serve to guide as negative illustrations.

      It is interesting how the Bible describes Jesus as the last Adam. Paul could have said the second Adam or some other term but instead he said Jesus is the *eschaton* Adam. This means he is the terminus of the line of Adam. If Jesus was merely the second Adam, Paul would have said that he was the *deuteros* Adam. However, Paul wants us to understand there had been a whole succession of Adams (individuals and corporate entities) who followed the first. For instance, the nation of Israel may be considered a second Adam.

King Saul is an example of a subsequent Adam. Like the first Adam, Saul is an example of how *not* to act. We learn from his example not by imitating it but by shunning it. We also learn through the contrast of his life with that of a godly man like David.

In this chapter, as we examine what it means to be men of Christ, we are going to look at the good example of King David, the bad example of King Saul and sum up with the idea that to know Jesus is to imitate him.

## *Relationship with Christ*

As we begin this discussion of what it means to be men of Christ I want to provide a brief summary of the life of David. Obviously we are not going to cover every detail but we will examine enough of David's history to recall how he was a type of Christ. In this overview we will consider what is in the life of David that was a reflection of Jesus Christ and what is therefore instructive concerning how *we* can be true men of Christ.

King David was a type of Christ and another man in the line of Adam as well. He showed the way to walk with the Lord but because he was only a type he was unable to fully demonstrate a life completely surrendered to God. He accomplished much and is called "a man after God's own heart" but he was not *the* Christ and so he was unable to bring the work of the kingdom to completion.

When we look at how David was chosen and anointed to be king it is clear it came about by the grace of God. In other words, David did nothing to bring about his election as the king of Israel. Prior to God choosing him, he was a simple shepherd in the region of Bethlehem - an undistinguished young man

*Men Of Issachar*

in an insignificant town in Judah.

As you recall, God told Samuel to go to Bethlehem to anoint a king from among the sons of Jesse. Samuel protested to the Lord saying, if Saul found out what he was doing, he would be killed. Thus, God told him to go and offer a sacrifice to Yahweh and to hold a festival for the townspeople. He was supposed to invite Jesse and his sons and then God would point out to him the man he had chosen to be the shepherd of his people.

So, Samuel went to Bethlehem and as the party progressed, the sons of Jesse are brought before him so that he might choose one to be king. When Samuel saw the oldest son of Jesse he thought "this must be God's chosen." After all, he was tall and good-looking. Evidently he was a warrior as well. And yet God said, "No, this is not the one." As we know, Samuel had all of the sons of Jesse (save one) promenade before him but none were chosen. Finally, Samuel asked Jesse "are all the young men here?" I bet Jesse was a little disappointed when none of his older sons had been chosen and he replied sheepishly (pun intended) *there remains yet the youngest, and there he is, keeping the sheep* (1 Samuel 16:11). Well, David was finally brought before Samuel and the Lord said, *Arise, anoint him; for this is the one!*

David was not the choice of the Prophet or even his own father; he was the choice of God himself. He was someone Samuel would have chosen because he was the youngest male in his family. As the youngest he was the least esteemed and would have the least influence. But it was God who chose David and he did so as an act of grace.

Once David was chosen as King, by implication he was given dominion. This is the same thing we see in the case of Adam. He was chosen (created) by God in grace. He did nothing to earn his creation anymore than David earned his anointing as king. Both of them were given dominion. Unlike Adam, David did not grasp for authority. David was a patient man. Not only did he go back to tending his sheep after having been selected as (future) King of Israel, he also endured many years of persecution at the hand of Saul.

We also see David serving the people. He began to serve the people by serving the king when he played his harp to sooth Saul's tormented spirit. He further served the masses and the king when he accepted the challenge of Goliath and killed the giant, using the monster's own sword to cut off his head. Here is a picture of the seed of the woman crushing the serpent's head. In this David succeeded where Adam failed. Adam failed to crush the serpent's head and so he failed as king and leader. David, however, was successful at this stage of the game.

The parallel between David and Jesus is evident in the persecution David endured. Just like Jesus Christ, David was persecuted by the king and the people. Jesus was persecuted by Herod, the Jewish leadership and ultimately by the people themselves. Like Jesus, David responded to this persecution with a show of patient strength. He kept himself out of harms way but he did nothing to retaliate.

Lest we think this is a minor accomplishment we should remember that the apostles of Jesus Christ initially didn't do as well. Christ had to restrain his apostles (James and John) when they wanted to call

*Men Of Issachar*

down fire on a Samaritan village that had refused hospitality to Jesus. Jesus rebuked them and told them they did not know what spirit they were representing. When Peter struck with the sword in defense of Jesus, the Lord rebuked him and healed the damaged ear of Peter's victim.

Even though David was persecuted by the people he continued to serve them. Throughout his "wilderness" wandering he and his motley band of outcasts found ample opportunity for David to hone his leadership skills and show interest in the people of Israel. For instance, the Philistines had attacked the city of Keilah. David inquired of the Lord saying, *shall I go up and attack these Philistines?* The Lord replied telling David to *go and attack the Philistines, and save Keilah* (1 Samuel 23:1-2). Yet even after David saved them from the brutality of the Philistines the men of Keilah were ready to deliver him into the hand of Saul.

Jesus did the same. He continually ministered to the children of Israel throughout Galilee, Judea and Jerusalem. However, at the end of his earthly ministry the people of Jerusalem cried out saying, "crucify him" for "we have no king but Caesar." They did this even though they had benefited from his works of power and heard his authoritative teaching.

David is also like Christ in the way he gathered a band of outcasts about him. Now, I'm not suggesting all the people who followed Jesus Christ were drawn from the dregs of society but we do know tax gatherers, prostitutes, zealots and malcontents gathered around Jesus. Even his chosen twelve were a rather ragged bunch.

David is also a good example in the way he

*Men Of Christ*

respected authority. He had two golden opportunities to rid himself of his tormentor but in both cases he said he would not lift his hand against God's anointed. He knew the time would come when he would be elevated to the throne but he was unwilling to take matters into his own hands. This is because David relied on God's direction. This was evident during his years of wandering but also when he became king. One time when the Philistines were preparing to attack Israel, David consulted the Lord on how to best conduct the battle. As you recall, God told David to attack first one way and then another - with both battles resulting in victory for Israel (2 Samuel 5:17-25).

Jesus had respect for authority as well. He was submitted to the Father and did not counsel his followers to rebel against the religious leaders. Instead he told them to do what they said (but not what they did), because they sat in Moses seat.

Probably the most important difference between David and Adam (and the most striking similarity between David and Christ) is David's willingness to wait upon the Lord for the promised kingship. Adam would have eventually been given the opportunity to eat of the tree of knowledge. This does not mean he would have been given the right to decide for himself what is right and wrong. It means that as God's vice regent he would have been entrusted with the authority to make decisions on his own. As he moved forward in wisdom and in his walk with God, his authority and responsibility would have been increased. However, Adam wanted authority immediately. Indeed, he wanted to strip God of sovereignty and determine for himself what was right and what was wrong - apart from God's

*Men Of Issachar*

standard of measure concerning morality. On the other hand, David was willing to wait for his opportunity to exercise authority as God's vice regent. He was not going to make decisions concerning right and wrong apart from God's divine guidance. It is true that David stumbled badly later in life and decided to create his own code of ethics. But that was not typical for him and as we know it brought tremendous heartache and hardship to the house of David.

We must also recognize the unifying power of David's reign. Until the time of the Kings, Israel was a highly decentralized people. Each tribe was a sovereign entity. Rather than a kingdom, Israel was a loosely confederated group of states. The Bible tells us this state of affairs was what God wanted. Yahweh did not want Israel to have a king other than himself. Nonetheless, in his sovereignty, God created the monarchy and used it to advance his eternal purpose for his people. And so, with the inauguration of David's kingdom we see a unity in Israel that had not previously existed. In fact, unity did not endure beyond the reign of King Solomon. This reminds us there can be no lasting unity apart from the ministry and the authority of Jesus Christ. But David, as a type of Christ, brought about a typical fulfillment of kingdom unity which exists only in Jesus.

Throughout his life David sought to honor God. He was not always successful because he was human and did things displeasing to Yahweh at times. Nevertheless he was a man who placed God first. Just like Jesus, he sought to do God's will not his own.

Moreover, David fought God's battles. In other words, he was not interested in expanding the borders of Israel simply for the sake of enlarging his own domain. His foreign wars were invariably defensive. David went on the offense only when he was seeking to rid the Promised Land of pagan inhabitants. This is also like Jesus Christ. Jesus fought the battles God wanted him to fight. He healed those whom the Father wanted healed. He used sharp words against those God wanted to rebuke. However, Jesus did not seek to create a domain of his own. He had every opportunity to do so but refused the popular demand to be king of Israel and take up arms against Rome.

Finally we recognize David as a type in the promise God gave him concerning the eternal nature of his house. This is fulfilled in Jesus Christ the true son of David and the true guarantor of the Davidic dynasty. It is significant that David's response to the promise of a dynasty was one of humility. Rather than rub his hands in glee while plotting the next move in the expansion of his kingdom he went in and sat humbly before God and expressed his amazement that the Creator of the universe would stoop to deal with one as lowly as he.

This is the crux of who David was. This is what is important about relationship with Almighty God. Indeed, as we will see, it is what is important about relationship with Jesus Christ.

### *Cannot Be Faked*

When we look at the life of King David there is much we can learn about what it means for us to be men of Christ. On the other hand, we eschew the example of Saul and learn how to better follow Jesus.

Like David, Saul was chosen by grace. Saul, stumbled into the kingship (from a human perspective) while he was out searching for his Father's lost

*Men Of Issachar*

donkeys. Yahweh told Samuel that he had chosen someone to be king and said he would send a particular man to his town that he might be anointed and recognized as the king of Israel. Thus, Saul wandered into Ramah with his servant looking for the seer in hopes he might be able to tell them where the donkeys were. To his surprise, Samuel the seer not only told him the donkeys had been found but that he was going to join Samuel at a sacrifice and feast. As the story continues, we find Saul spent the night at Samuel's house and was anointed king of Israel the next day.

Again, there was no work, no striving for the kingdom. Indeed, when he was confronted with Samuel's announcement of his new role, Saul protested. He said he was a nobody from the smallest tribe in Israel.

Once again we see parallels with the experience of Adam. Adam was chosen by grace and given dominion – chosen to be the vice regent of Almighty God. Unfortunately the parallel with Adam does not end there. It wasn't long before Saul decided he knew better than God and began to make decisions concerning right and wrong independent of Yahweh and his prophet.

Initially, Saul was a good king. He rallied the people of Israel and early in his reign he brought unity to the confederation of independent tribes. But as Saul became accustomed to the privileges of authority he lost his former humility and grew in pride and self-centeredness.

It is interesting that Saul was given a helper just as Adam had been given a helper. Obviously, in this case it was not a woman created from matter scooped from his side. Instead, it was the young man

David who came along side the king. He helped Saul in his role by providing music to soothe his troubled mind, in defeating the monster Goliath and as a commander of Israel's armies.

Nonetheless, Saul failed to protect his helper. Indeed, Saul attempted to destroy him. I am not saying Adam attempted to destroy his helper Eve but he failed to protect her and so brought ruin upon himself. The same can be said of Saul. Rather than protect his helper and nurture his abilities to the benefit of the kingdom, Saul eventually attempted to kill David. First he tried to have David killed in battle and when that failed he took direct action against his assistant.

Like Adam, king Saul blamed his right-hand for his woes. When David returned from the battle in which Goliath was killed and many of the Philistines slaughtered, the women came out to meet the returning army singing, "Saul has killed his thousands and David his tens of thousands." Instead of rejoicing in the victory God had brought through the ministry of the king's helper, Saul grew jealous and suggested David's real intent was to seize the throne. This further damaged Saul's ability to protect those under his authority. In his attempts to destroy David, Saul began to neglect the rest of the nation and instead of guarding the borders of Israel he would often be found traipsing around the countryside in search of his son-in-law. One result of this falling from grace was the unraveling of the fragile unity of the nation of Israel. As Saul bent his every energy toward destroying David he introduced a rift into the national consciousness that never healed.

As Saul progressed down the path Adam had traveled, he began to ignore God's word in any in-

*Men Of Issachar*

stance it proved to be inconvenient. For instance, when God commanded him to destroy the Amalekites, Saul decided it would be better to spare some of the livestock and the king as well. Saul displayed another aspect of Adam's character in that situation; he listened to the voice of the people and then tried to blame *them* for his failure (1 Samuel 15:1-23). In the same way, Adam listened to the voice of his wife and then tried to blame her for his failure. Moreover, Saul attempted to excuse his behavior by appealing to the provision of privilege in his relationship with God. In other words, Saul said he had spared the livestock so he might worship God with sacrifices. Adam also appealed to God's provision when he said "the woman whom you gave to be with me, she gave me of the tree, and I ate." In both cases an attempt was made to blame God. After all, if God had not made a woman - or had not allowed for sacrifices - "none of this would have happened." In both cases men who had been given authority as God's vice regent failed to lead and failed to protect simply because they thought they knew better than God.

     Eventually Saul was displaced. He was barred from God's presence and found it impossible to receive direction from Yahweh. At his lowest point, Saul sought out the witch of Endor in an attempt to contact the departed Samuel. Ironically, God did allow Samuel to speak from the grave - much to the surprise and consternation of the witch. All of this was to no avail; Saul was killed in battle and his rule given to another. This, again, is not unlike the experience of Adam. Adam was killed in a spiritual sense and his rule was given to the very one he had allowed to seduce his helper.

*Men Of Christ*

## *To Know Is To Imitate*

Men of Christ can learn from David's positive example and the negative example of Saul. In the first place all of us are chosen by grace to be in union with the Father in Christ. As it says in Ephesians 2:8-10, *For by grace you have been saved through faith, and that not of yourselves; it is the gift of God, not of works, lest anyone should boast. For we are His workmanship, created in Christ Jesus for good works, which God prepared before-hand that we should walk in them.* Every Christian man begins his journey as a chosen one. This is true for every Christian but I want to focus on the fact that *men* of Christ are chosen and created in Christ Jesus for good works that God prepared beforehand to walk in.

In other words, we are chosen as men of Christ and given a particular set of works *we* must accomplish as part of our salvation. I'm not suggesting we earn our salvation through those works; I am saying that part of the gracious gift of God in salvation is a new type of behavior. As men of Christ, that behavior most especially includes our duty as husbands and fathers.

Just as it was with Adam we have been given dominion. Of course we do not want to exercise the authority we have been given in the way Adam or Saul did. We want to exercise dominion in the way David and Jesus did. Our blueprint for exercising this authority is found in God's Word.

As Christian men we are vice regents given the responsibility to exercise the rule of Jesus Christ in our own life and arena of activity. It is critical for men of Christ to learn to exercise authority in their own life before they attempt to do so in a family. Single Christian men need to bring their life under

*Men Of Issachar*

the authority of Jesus Christ so they will be prepared to be servant leaders as husbands and fathers. This is something we need to understand as Believers. A man may be ready for marriage at age 20 or he may be ready at age 30. The criteria are not limited to his chronological age but the exercise of authority in his own life. A Christian man must first learn to "lead" himself and learn to walk even as Jesus walked.

Thus men of Christ must be patient. Not only patient as they await God's timing for marriage and family but patient once they become husbands and fathers. Christian men must not grasp for greater authority than the Lord has given. Obviously, by the time a man is married he has leadership thrust upon him and forbearance in exercising authority will be different at that point then in the case of a single man of Christ.

Once a man has a wife (and children in God's time) he is responsible for exercising servant leadership in his own household. In a previous chapter I mentioned that talk of male leadership and male authority often makes people uncomfortable because we have an erroneous understanding of leadership and authority. I cited Jesus' words to his apostles concerning kingdom leadership. In the passage from Mark (10:35-45), Jesus contrasts kingdom authority with worldly leadership. The world describes the use of authority as service, but it rarely is. Instead, leadership of a worldly kind is domineering. Rather than seek the last place and act as a servant to those being led, the world considers taking the first place and being served as characteristics of leadership.

Men of Christ must learn to be servant leaders willing to lay their life down for those they lead. They must be willing to provide an example of service in word and in deed. They must be willing to be peacemakers rather than always be "right." They must be willing to forgo their own desire in order to care for those under their authority. It doesn't matter whether we feel like doing so or not. A servant leader is strong enough to think of others more highly than himself even when it is inconvenient and uncomfortable.

We must also recognize, as married men, God has given each of us a special helper. A man of Christ must seek to nurture his wife and help her to grow in Christlikeness. Even though this is an act of service toward another it will ultimately be for a man's own benefit. I have found this to be the case in my life time and time again. We cannot be like Saul who grew jealous of the success of his helper. Obviously, the relationship between Saul and David was different from that of a man and his wife but the principle remains the same. Saul was given David as a helper. Men of Christ are given wives as helpers. And when our helper matures in Christ and begins to express what it is God has made her - those good works which God prepared beforehand that she should walk in - we should rejoice in her spiritual maturation. It would be the height of foolishness for a man to grow envious of his helper. Instead we need to understand that in the covenant of marriage the two are made one and her success is ours just as our success is hers.

At the same time you cannot be guilty of allowing your helper to lead. In other words, you cannot place your responsibility for leadership upon the shoulders of your wife. It may appear that her Christlikeness comes much more easily than your own but it would be wrong for you to assume that allows you the privilege of abdicating your role as leader. Invariably when Christian men do this they end up blaming their helper for their own spiritual woes. When men fail to obey God's command to lead it is typical to look for a scape-goat. It becomes easy to blame someone else for our disinterest in leadership or inability to connect the dots in the puzzle of bringing the rule of Jesus Christ to bear in our arena of activity.

Part of our leadership as men entails bringing unity to our household. We will not always be successful in this. Every human being must choose to follow Jesus Christ on their own and sometimes men of Christ will have children who walk away from the faith. However, if we do our job properly that will be a rare circumstance. In any event our duty is to honor God in all things. As David and Jesus did before us, we must give priority to God's will. Therefore, we cannot compromise in order to create the facade of family unity.

It is also important for us to lead as one who respects authority. We cannot expect to be effective leaders if we thumb our nose at authority. The Bible tells us that all authority is given by God and clearly says church and civil leadership must be respected. This doesn't mean we are bound to always agree with ecclesiastical or civic leaders but even our disagreement must be respectful and submissive.

As it was in the ministry of Jesus Christ, men of Christ must be willing to suffer persecution. We probably won't be beaten or stoned by angry mobs if we attempt to exercise leadership in our arena of activity; the persecution I'm speaking of is the skepticism we might face as we attempt to walk as Jesus walked. At that point it would be very easy to began to blame those under our authority for our inability to express Christ in our role as leader. That would be the worst mistake we could make. That would be like Adam or Saul. Instead, we want to be like David or Jesus and continue to serve those under our authority even if they do not show appreciation for our effort.

As men of Christ we may be called to exercise leadership at our own peril. It may be that the peril is found within our own family. Again, I don't mean our life will be in danger; it may be that the relationships in our family and sphere of influence are stressed. I have already mentioned my Father's example. There was a time in the life of our family when my Dad began to lead his family down a doctrinal path that caused a certain amount of friction in the family. It was the right way to go but it was not a comfortable direction to move. A lesser man would have backed away from the evidence of peril and refused to lead any further. However, Dad was man enough to understand that part of his duty as a Christian husband and father was to lead even when it brought turmoil to the household.

We may even face peril in our community as we begin to exercise leadership. This might seem far-fetched but that is primarily because we often fail to live like those who truly serve the Messiah. It is very easy to go with the flow but when we start to swim upstream we make other people uncomfortable. I don't know what we might face as men of Christ who are willing to lead as Jesus would lead but we must be willing to continue to exercise servant leadership even when it rocks the boat. As Paul wrote, *every one who is determined to live a godly life as a follower of Christ Jesus will be persecuted*

*Men Of Issachar*

(2 Timothy 3:12)

This brings me to another idea I need to mention. It is important to fight God's battles and not our own. In other words, servant leadership will sometimes require us to decide what hill we are willing to die on. There is a multitude of problems in society that need correction but we are not obligated to fight every battle. Each individual's theater of warfare is limited and we must be sure we pick the fight God wants us to fight. There are some enemy battlements inviting attack that are common to the campaign of every leader; there are others that are one man's alone. Even then men of Christ must gather a platoon of like-minded Christians to participate in the conflict. None of us are supposed to charge the enemy without backup.

As Christian men we are members of the eternal dynasty of the Son of Man. This knowledge should strengthen us in our task and encourage us as we realize the victory of the kingdom does not depend upon our feeble efforts. Rather, Christ is the victor and we have been called to join him in his victory. Our job is to do our very best as men of Christ and leave the results to him. We can rest assured that if we truly walk as Jesus walked we will see success in our exercise of servant leadership.

We can only do these things as we are empowered by the Holy Spirit. We must be guided in our leadership every step of the way. We have the word of God that provides the blueprint and we have the Holy Spirit within us who gives us the strength. Paul tells us it is God who gives us both the desire and the ability to do his will (Philippians 2:12-13). Therefore, our efforts to provide leadership in our family and arena of activity must be bathed in prayer.

We cannot attempt to do things our own way. We must never attempt to try and exercise authority according to our own standard of right and wrong.
### *Conclusion*
In the next three chapters we will begin to look at the way men of Christ are supposed to carry out servant leadership. In chapter four we will see that men of Christ must understand the times. Chapter five initiates an examination of the duties of Christian men while chapter six continues the investigation. At this point in our study, I encourage you to seek God's face and ask for the desire to lead. I encourage you to rearrange your thinking. I enjoin you to consider your role as a man of Christ and urge you to study the Bible so you might discover what it means to be a servant leader in imitation of Jesus Christ.

I am fully convinced we will not see positive, lasting change in the Family, church or society until men of Christ embrace their duty to imitate Jesus and be servant leaders. The first step is to understand we have been given the responsibility to lead. The second step is to act upon it. May our Lord Jesus Christ convince us of our duty and empower us to carry it through.

# Chapter 4
## Understand the Times

*The ox knows its owner, and the donkey its master's crib, but Israel does not know, my people do not understand* (Isaiah 1:3 English Standard Version)

A man cannot be content to be a follower of Jesus in word only. Men of Christ must be men. They cannot be satisfied with the namby-pamby Christianity that has been the norm in too many Churches for too long. To be a true Christian man requires work; it requires a certain amount of physical work but before that it requires plenty of mental work.

Men of Christ cannot be lax in the arena of intellectual development. Certainly it is more than mere "cerebral ontogenesis;" it is godly wisdom and understanding we seek. Nevertheless, Christian men cannot neglect the duty of intelligent involvement in this life and realm.

Leadership based on personal charisma or a "will to power" will eventually falter in the face of opposition. The man who has an understanding of the Bible, of God and of himself will lead as he should.

*Understand The Times*

A man who understands something of the past, present and future is the one who will be able to provide godly leadership. It is understanding in this broad sense that will guide the leadership of a man of Christ and enable him to do the job God has called him to do as a husband, father, worker, manager, community leader or legislator.

***Understand The Bible***

The source of true understanding is the Holy Spirit and the Spirit's instruction book is the Bible. Indeed, the Word of God is more than this; it is a point of contact between heaven and earth. In it are the very words of God as recorded by servants of the Almighty as inspired by the Holy Spirit. Thus, the only way to understand the Bible is to have the Holy Spirit open our eyes and our ears.

Dry knowledge of the contents of Scripture will not somehow give us the understanding we need in order to be suitable leaders. We should be careful of the trap of humanistic intellectualism. If we understand the Bible, we understand true faith as intellectual assent, emotional response and action (see, D. Eric Williams, *Real Faith: Studies In The Epistle Of James*). It is not possible to separate any one of these three components from the equation and still have real faith. Modern Americans tend to divide, slice and dissect everything into its smallest possible parts but that really cannot be done with faith.

In the final analysis, faith is about obedience. But it is obedience that springs from a heart warmed by an understanding of truth. Therefore, merely going through the motions because it is acceptable in your circle of friends is inadequate. A true man of Christ works at developing his understanding be-

*Men Of Issachar*

cause he is wholly devoted to his Lord and Savior Jesus Christ. Like the soldier who would go through hell for a superior officer he esteems, we must be warriors who are willing to do whatever it takes to be the men that Christ demands.

The understanding we hope to develop is a wisdom enabling us to act in godliness. In other words, we hope to cultivate the ability to think as God thinks. This means we will be able to look at the circumstances around us – in our own life, in our family, in our church and community – and read the situation as God would read it. Our goal should be to arrive at the place where we have the mind of Christ in such evidence that our judgment is sought out by others concerning the issues of the day. This is one way we will know we have adequate understanding to lead.

The best way to understand the Bible is to read it. That doesn't mean you should pick it up when we have nothing else to do and casually thumb through a few pages. You must have a well ordered approach to his Bible reading. You must read the Bible and you must read it a lot. The best approach to systematic Bible reading I know of is an old Puritan method that enables the reader to encounter all parts of the Bible every week. It works like this:

| | |
|---|---|
| Monday: | Three chapters from Genesis to Deuteronomy. |
| Tuesday: | Three chapters from Joshua to 2 Kings. |
| Wednesday: | Three chapters from 1 Chronicles to Job. |
| Thursday: | Three chapters from Psalms to Song of Solomon. |
| Friday: | Three chapters from Isaiah to |

|           | Malachi.                        |
| Saturday: | Three chapters from Matthew to Acts. |
| Sunday:   | Three chapters from Romans to Revelation. |

If you have the time, I would suggest you read a portion from each of these sections on a daily basis. At the very least, every man should commit to reading according to the weekly schedule outlined above.

Scripture displays the character of God in several literary genres. Historical accounts show how he deals with mankind in this time space reality. Some of the examples will be positive - men of God who did what they were supposed to do and walked in fellowship with the creator. But we will also encounter negative examples that reveal the way God deals with those who hold him at a distance and refuse to obey him.

The Bible also contains hero stories and epic tales. The Bible challenges us with poetry, Psalms and prophecy. Scripture invites us to think through the dark sayings of Proverbs and other wisdom literature. In all of this, a man of Christ will grow to know the one whom he serves, the one we call Father, Son and Holy Spirit. A man will come to understand something of God's plan for creation and why he brought the universe into being. Just so you understand a bit of what I am talking about, the whole purpose of this realm we call creation is to bring glory to God and to showcase the person and work of the Eternal Son. The Bible is given to equip us to "carry forward his purposes of new covenant and new creation" (see, N. T. Wright, *Simply Christian: Why Christianity Makes Sense).*

We develop an ability to *make use* of understanding as we put it into practice in our own life and family first. This is why the Bible says a man who was unable to keep his own household in line should not be in leadership in the church. If his family is out-of-order, it tells us he has not developed the kind of understanding and leadership a man of Christ should have. And, if he has not developed that ability in the most basic aspect of his responsibility he should not be given additional responsibility.

In this day and age of specialization and the segregation of knowledge it is common to suggest a man cannot have understanding concerning all things. In the broadest sense this is true. You may not know everything there is to know about a particular subject such as nuclear physics unless you study that field. However, as a man of Christ who has developed the mind of God in your own life and has gained in biblical understanding, you *will* have wisdom that can speak to every aspect of life. In other words, a man of Christ with godly wisdom can certainly speak to issues that impact the realm of nuclear physics. Godly wisdom is not limited to issues of family or personal piety or ecclesiastical circumstance. Instead, *he who is spiritual judges all things, yet he himself is rightly judged by no one. For "WHO HAS KNOWN THE MIND OF THE LORD THAT HE MAY INSTRUCT HIM?" But we have the mind of Christ* (1 Corinthians 2:15-16).

A man of Christ who has developed godly wisdom will possess understanding allowing him to judge any situation he may encounter. Obviously, most of us will be limited in our arena of activity to subjects with which we are quite familiar. Yet, we should not think biblical knowledge and understanding have a narrow application. *Every* human endeavor is subject to the authority of God. *Everything* in this realm must be examined by the mind of God and be reconciled to the will of the Almighty. We may not understand all of the technical details (unless trained in the discipline) but the wisdom of God within us enables us to address every circumstance in fundamental (worldview) terms and thus to provide leadership.

Men of Christ need to recognize their responsibility. The world cries out for leadership. Creation is begging for men of Christ to take the lead; instead, *the earnest expectation of the creation eagerly waits for the revealing of the sons of God. For the creation was subjected to futility, not willingly, but because of Him who subjected it in hope; because the creation itself also will be delivered from the bondage of corruption into the glorious liberty of the children of God. For we know that the whole creation groans and labors with birth pangs together until now* (Romans 8:19-22).

## Understand God

Obviously, a man cannot have a true understanding of God unless he is born again. Even then his discernment is limited. Still, the Bible and the Holy Spirit enable us to "make contact" with the Almighty in an authentic way.

Our apprehension of God must be based upon the presupposition that the Bible is a wholly reliable source of information concerning our Father in heaven. Based upon our understanding of human nature, we recognize that those who are not in Jesus Christ will belittle our stand for truth, telling us it is wholly illogical to presuppose the truth of the Bible. As men of under-standing we must be able to explain to them why our *a priori* reasoning is far less

*Men Of Issachar*

ridiculous than their presuppositions concerning the unreliability of the Bible. Anyone with a modicum of common sense should look at creation and come to the conclusion that there is a designer. There are a number of books on the subject that point out the foolishness of suggesting that all of this came into being by accident (see for instance, *Darwin's Black Box*, by Michael Behe, *Evolution: Theory in Crisis*, and *Nature's Destiny* both by Michael Denton). In any case, men of Christ must not be embarrassed by the fact they *presuppose* the Bible to be authoritative.

To understand God, we must understand the Eternal Son, Jesus Christ. As our Lord said, "*If you really knew me, you would know my Father as well. From now on, you do know him and have seen him.*" *Philip said, "Lord, show us the Father and that will be enough for us." Jesus answered: "Don't you know me, Philip, even after I have been among you such a long time? Anyone who has seen me has seen the Father. How can you say, 'Show us the Father'? Don't you believe that I am in the Father, and that the Father is in me? The words I say to you are not just my own. Rather, it is the Father, living in me, who is doing his work*" (John 14:7-10). We must make it our aim to study the life of Christ as presented to us in the scripture. Moreover, we need to strive to walk even as he walked (1 John 2:6), for in learning to imitate him we best learn about him.

It is critical to understand God (to the extent he has allowed us through creation and his revealed word) in order to properly lead. Those who take time to truly get to know the Lord will be enabled to truly represent him.

*Understand The Times*

## *Understand Self*

In his *Institutes Of The Christian Religion,* John Calvin suggests the first step in general understanding is to know oneself. He begins his *Institutes* with a brief chapter devoted to the topic of knowing God by knowing ourselves. He says "our wisdom, in so far as it ought to be deemed true and solid wisdom, consists almost entirely of two parts: knowledge of God and of ourselves" (see, John Calvin, *The Institutes Of The Christian Religion*, 1:1:1). Calvin means no man can survey himself without soon turning his thoughts to God. This of course must be understood in light of the illumination of the Holy Spirit. The unsaved man may consider who and what he is but according to the book of Romans, such self-examination will end with an attempt to hold down the innate knowledge of God and the denial of the obvious. In other words, no one can be reasoned into the kingdom of God. Calvin is right to say the wonder of human complexity is sure evidence of the existence of Yahweh as creator. Yet, this will not cause the unbeliever to turn his face to God in repentance. Instead, left to his own resources, he plunges deeper into sin in an effort to drown out the nagging voice of conscience. Only when the Holy Spirit enlightens a man's mind is he able to espouse the handiwork of God in his own being and in the creation around him. Without the Holy Spirit, unrighteous men will sup-press the truth in unrighteousness, *because what may be known of God is manifest in them, for God has shown it to them. For since the creation of the world His invisible attributes are clearly seen, being understood by the things that are made, even His eternal power and Godhead, so that they are with-*

*out excuse, because, although they knew God, they did not glorify Him as God, nor were thankful, but became futile in their thoughts, and their foolish hearts were darkened. Professing to be wise, they became fools* (Romans 1:19-22).

Thus, the Christian, in contemplating his own person, has his eyes turned to God. Empowered by the Holy Spirit, he will recognize he is the handiwork of God and understand he does not measure up to the standard of God's holy word. This is why Calvin spends very little time on the subject before he plunges into a discussion concerning the character of God as displayed in creation and in holy writ.

I believe knowledge about ourselves and God will grow in tandem. As a Christian man seeks to know more about his God he will naturally learn more about himself. For instance, he will come to understand that no man can have a relationship with the creator of the universe apart from Jesus Christ. He will understand that as a descendant of Adam, he is born in sin. Not only does he have a sin nature he will admit he is a sinner in his own right. Therefore, a man of Christ must know himself. He must know and understand who he is in the sight of God; first as one who was apart from God and then as one who is in relationship with God in Jesus Christ. This is important because he needs to recognize the circumstance of his fellow human beings. In other words, a Christian man must know that before he was in relationship with Jesus Christ he was a sinner destined for eternal punishment and now, as a man of Christ, he is destined for eternal relationship. Indeed, that eternal relationship began the moment he was born again.

To be an effective leader, a man of Christ

needs a clear understanding of the condition of humanity. It is important for a Christian man to understand who he is so he might understand humanity as a whole. He must recognize that people are not naturally good but depraved and touched by the stain of sin in every aspect of their being. He should also have a clear view of what happens when a person comes to a saving knowledge of Jesus Christ. Both of these are critical issues for the man who hopes to lead. Anyone who thinks human beings are naturally good and are simply a product of their environment will fail in the realm of leadership - be it in their own home or in the community. This is why it is so important for men of Christ to begin with an understanding of themselves and by extension, of the human race.

Another way a Christian men ought to understand himself is in an accurate assessment of his abilities and gifting. I'm not suggesting you should get caught up in the ever popular "find your spiritual gift" craze or anything of that sort. Simple life-experience will reveal what a man is good at and what he has a passion for. It isn't any more complicated than that. For instance, a man may have a passion for football but his athletic talent is limited to the ability to drag extra chairs into the living-room for his buddies when they come over to watch the big game. Under these circumstances he should realize God did not create him for a professional football career. However, he may have made him for some other activity in the domain of sports: coach, manager, marketing agent or whatever.

A man of Christ needs to discover where he can be most effective for the kingdom. Every part of life is to be brought under the lordship of Jesus

*Men Of Issachar*

Christ and so the Lord has made men of every sort to do the job. Some are managers, some artisans, some communicators and others musically inclined. Each man should determine where he fits into God's scheme as he prayerfully evaluates his talents, interests and experience. If a fellow is having some trouble discovering his kingdom calling he can solicit the advice of those who know him best (wife, pastor, friends).

Another issue to understand is that you may not make your living from your calling. Moreover, your calling may not be exercised in an ecclesiastical setting. For instance, a man might have the gift of administration but that doesn't mean he will be employed in full-time church work. More likely, he will be employed elsewhere as he labors to bring his arena of activity under the lordship of Jesus Christ. Remember, there is no division between sacred and secular in the kingdom of God.

It doesn't matter whether or not you think you are particularly gifted. Each man must realize he has been created in Christ Jesus for good works (Ephesians 2:10). It is simply good stewardship to recognize your natural and spiritual gifts and make use of them in the messianic kingdom.

A first step is to accept that you cannot be anything you want to be. Instead you must realize you are a unique individual made for a unique purpose. The Bible says, *For I say, through the grace given to me, to everyone who is among you, not to think of himself more highly than he ought to think, but to think soberly, as God has dealt to each one a measure of faith. For as we have many members in one body, but all the members do not have the same function, so we, being many, are one body in Christ, and individually members of one another. Having then gifts differing according to the grace that is given to us, let us use them: if prophecy, let us prophesy in proportion to our faith; or ministry, let us use it in our ministering; he who teaches, in teaching; he who exhorts, in exhortation; he who gives, with liberality; he who leads, with diligence; he who shows mercy, with cheerfulness* (Romans 12:3-8). In other words, every Christian man is called to function within the parameters of their God given endowments. When they do so, they bring their arena of responsibility under the lordship of Christ as they ought (this doesn't mean there won't be any difficulty in doing so).

Our duty to understand does not end with a grasp of the Bible, God and ourselves. As we touched on in the first chapter, a man of Christ also needs to understand the times. This insight should focus on the family, the church and the state

### *Understand The Family*

Family may be described as "the collective body of persons who live in one house and under one head or manager; a household, including parents, children and servants, and as the case may be, lodgers or boarders" (see, Noah Webster's 1828 *Dictionary of American English)*. But according to the Bible it is God who created the family and so it is God who defines it. Scripture tells us, in the beginning God created male and female - *both* in the image of God. This is where the family began. The creation principle remained in force even in the days of Noah after the flood; a man and wife - and in the case of Noah, children - exemplify family. This is what we see in Scripture; a man and a woman come together to make a family. Certainly if a man and woman are so blessed, their family will include children but that is up to the Lord himself.

Therefore, a family is defined as a husband and wife and those who are part of their household, under their authority. The family is not defined on the basis of the clan. God said a man should leave his mother and father and cleave to his wife. Jesus Christ affirmed this. Hence, the idea that the clan constitutes the family is not scriptural, even though the sentiment is common among many Christians today. For instance, there is the view that a grown child should remain in the same region as the "tribe" in order to maintain clan cohesion. On one hand there is nothing wrong with this. It's a fine idea to have a good relationship with your extended family but that relationship cannot get in the way of your duty as a husband and father. Jesus himself said, if a man does not hate his mother and his Father, his wife and his children and so on, he is not fit for the kingdom of God. In other words, a man cannot allow any relationship - including the family-clan relationship - to stand in the way of his responsibility as a follower of Jesus Christ and part of that responsibility is to leave father and mother and cleave to his wife.

The Genesis record also provides the purpose of the family unit. That purpose is dominion. Dominion or stewardship under the headship of Almighty God includes the duty of procreation. You may not like to define the sexual relationship you enjoy with your wife as a duty but in a very real sense it is. It is an extremely pleasurable duty but a duty of the Christian man nonetheless. Families - men and women joined in covenant relationship - have the responsibility to bring children into this world in order to better fulfill the dominion mandate. As the saying goes, many hands make light work and that adage is applicable to the task of dominion. Scripture tells us the man of God who has many sons will not fear his enemies in the gate. Our enemies don't hang around the gate in the 21$^{st}$ century but a man of Christ can expect to suffer persecution if he lives godly in Christ Jesus (2 Timothy 3:12). I know from personal experience that a house full of godly children is a bulwark against the pressure of the world. There is strength in numbers when those numbers are all walking in righteousness. A man of Christ should have a strong desire for children whom he may bring into the work of the kingdom alongside his own labors.

Realize that a "family" has a particular composition. It is made up of a husband and wife and children as God so blesses but must be structured in a particular way. According to the Bible, the husband is the head of the household. A wife is to respect her husband and the two of them together make up a single unit working to bring the kingdom of God to bear in their sphere of influence. Moreover, both have the duty to equip their children to do the same. A properly structured family will "image" the trinitarian relationship. There will be an equality of worth or perhaps we might say an equality of essence but different roles within the family unit. My primary point is that the husband is the head of the house and that a husband and wife form a single unit designed to bring the kingdom of God to bear in their domain of responsibility. Part of the obligation in bringing the kingdom to bear in an arena of activity is to raise children who can duplicate and indeed improve upon the work of their

*Men Of Issachar*

parents.

The family is where basic training for the kingdom takes place. This is true for the husband and the wife as well as for the children. We understand this is so because the track record of a man in his own household is of primary importance in choosing men for leadership within the church. Thus, the family is a proving ground for the man of Christ as he learns to exercise servant leadership. As he does this he will bring his wife and children to a place where they are better able to image Christ to the world. The family unit is the most visible and accessible example of the kingdom of God. Families are everywhere and all people are familiar with the idea of "family." On the other hand, many people would never set foot inside a church building. They think of church as a place where people wear sour expressions and talk about hellfire and brimstone. While the church has a primary role in expanding the kingdom of God through her prophetic ministry (more on that later), the family unit operating under the authority of Jesus Christ is an approachable example of the kingdom easily grasped and digested by the non-Christian. Therefore, the unbeliever can look at a smoothly functioning kingdom family and be drawn to ask questions that will open a door for the man of Christ and those under his charge to share the gospel of Jesus. The family unit expressing the authority of Jesus Christ in their arena of activity is the best advertizement for the King of Kings.

A man should understand he has a *duty* to establish a family as God so allows. A man of Christ should not willingly remain single unless it is a ministry God has called him to. Paul says some folks are called to remain unmarried in the kingdom of

God but that is not the norm. Therefore, an unmarried Christian man not called to celibacy will desire to abandon his self-centered singleness and be proactive in seeking out a wife; yet even this is in God's timing.

The married man of Christ must recognize his position as head of the household and guide to those under his charge. In the following chapters we will talk about his specific responsibilities but at this point I will simply say a man has the duty to guide, protect, nurture and to seek the success of his wife and children. He has the duty to establish the identity of his family as an outpost of the kingdom and to work to extend his family's influence.

### Understand The Church

The true church began with God's choice of Abraham and in the covenant promise established between Abraham and the creator of the universe. Reliant upon his own counsel and no other, God determined that through Abraham all the earth would be blessed and all of the covenant promises would be realized in Abraham's seed.

But not everyone who carried the blood of Abraham in their veins was among the chosen people. They were physically part of the chosen race established in Abraham, Isaac and Jacob, but as the apostle Paul says, *all who are Israel are not Israel* (Romans 9:6). The history of Israel shows that from the very beginning most of the people were ungodly and unrepentant. Only those who trusted in God and walked in obedience were "truly saved" and they were always in the minority.

It was from this remnant that the Messiah arose. Born of the tribe of Judah, Son of Jacob, son of Isaac, son of Abraham, Jesus is the one true seed of Abraham (Galatians 3:16) and according to the apostle Paul, it is in him that all the covenant promises of God are "yes" (2 Corinthians 1:20).

During his earthly ministry Jesus gathered together the remnant of faithful Israel and established the church of the new covenant age. This is not evidence of discontinuity between the old and the new covenants, but a maturing of the old covenant and fulfillment of all the Law and the Prophets in Jesus Christ, the *embodiment* of the new covenant. The church as we know it today is a continuation of the body of believers who have remained faithful to Yahweh throughout many generations. With Christ's birth, life, death, resurrection, ascension and evidence of his enthronement in the outpouring of the Spirit on the day of Pentecost, the new covenant church, the body of Jesus Christ, came into being.

Jesus Christ and the church are inseparably united. The church cannot exist apart from the Lord Jesus; he is the head and we are the Body. As the head, Jesus has unconditional control over the body and is the supreme authority over the church. In this relationship, the church shares in the resurrection life and power of Jesus the Lord. The church is victorious because her head is victorious. The church has true power because Jesus the Christ has *all* power.

The church is called the Bride of Jesus Christ and the Lord is a faithful husband who laid his life down for his Bride in his death on the cross. He continues to serve his Bride, watching over her and bringing her to perfection.

Although the church is called the Bride of Jesus Christ, we must recognize there are members of the institution who are not spiritually joined to

*Understand The Times*

Jesus. There are people who are Christians on the outside but not truly born-again. They partake of the blessings of the Bride through their association with the institution of the church but on that final day their faith will be found wanting when it is revealed that they have not experienced the new birth. Only those who have been called into relationship with Almighty God in Jesus Christ by the power of the Holy Spirit are members of the visible and the invisible church alike. God has chosen for himself a people out of humanity and joined them together as one Body, the church. Thus within that entity which people generally see as the church, there are genuine believers along with those who have no true faith in Christ. Often it is difficult to differentiate between the two and ultimately only God knows the difference.

We often think of the church in terms of a local Body. This is fine as long as we realize each localized expression of Christ's Body is part of a whole and must be in fellowship with that whole in order to be a functioning part of the church. This does not mean every church must be a member of one denomination or another, but it is inappropriate for a local fellowship to be "a denomination of one." Just as individual Believers are joined one to another in the Body of Christ, likewise each demonstration of Christ's Bride must be in fellowship with the other representatives of the church.

The Bible is not entirely clear concerning the polity of the local church. It is apparent that each local body should be governed by elders and deacons and it appears the various localized fellowships ought to be under the oversight of local or perhaps regional authority. Our primary concern in this book is the structure of authority in the local body.

The Bible tells us the church must be governed by men who have proven themselves as leaders of their own household. As the apostle Paul says, *An elder must be such a good man that no one can rightly criticize him. He must be faithful to his wife. He must have self-control and be wise. He must be respected by others. He must be ready to help people by welcoming them into his home. He must be a good teacher. He must not drink too much, and he must not be someone who likes to fight. He must be gentle and peaceful. He must not be someone who loves money. He must be a good leader of his own family. This means that his children obey him with full respect. If a man does not know how to lead his own family, he will not be able to take care of God's church. An elder must not be a new believer. It might make him too proud of himself. Then he would be condemned for his pride the same as the devil was. An elder must also have the respect of people who are not part of the church. Then he will not be criticized by others and be caught in the devil's trap* (1 Timothy 3:2-7, ERV). If a man does not meet the biblical standard, he is not qualified to be an elder. Period. Only those who are qualified should be given the responsibility to watch over the flock.

Elders will teach and administer the sacraments while deacons are responsible for the practical aspects of ministry. Under the headship of both elders and deacons, the church involves itself in the work of the kingdom: preaching the gospel, disciplining believers and ministering to the poor, sick, hungry and victims of injustice.

In addition to elders and deacons there are

other ministries of service within the church. Evangelists, pastors and teachers, administrators, helpers and so on must be given oversight and nurtured in the ways of the kingdom. Like any good parent or manager, elders are required to discern the gifts and abilities of the flock and to help individual Christians - and the corporate body - maximize their potential in the work of the kingdom.

Finally, every Christian is required to be part of a corporate expression of Christ's body. No person can be a "church of one" and claim to be a Believer. A Believer is defined "in part" as a member of the body of Jesus Christ. And a member of the body of Jesus Christ is, by definition, attached to a local church.

## Understand The State

The third primary area of interest to the man of Christ is the civic realm. There are those who would suggest Christian men should not soil their hands by participating in politics. This betrays a lack of understanding concerning the nature of the kingdom of God. As we have discussed elsewhere, the kingdom of God is all about the rule of Jesus Christ. As we know from Scripture, the rule and reign of Jesus Christ began with his earthly ministry and will never end. Moreover, the Bible clearly states that all things are under the authority of Christ. Jesus him-self said all authority in heaven and earth had been given to him (Matthew 28:18-20) and that his followers are to make disciples of all nations, teaching them to obey all he commanded. No aspect of life is exempt from the oversight of the reigning king of the universe. This is true for those who serve as civil magistrates as much as for anyone else. Indeed, the Bible clearly states civil leaders are servants of God and as such they are bound to obey him in the discharge of their duties: *For [civil] government is God's servant to you for good. But if you do wrong, be afraid, because it does not carry the sword for no reason. For government is God's servant, an avenger that brings wrath on the one who does wrong* (Romans 13:4 HCSB). Therefore, it is important for a man of Christ to grasp certain things about politics.

This is not to suggest politics are primary. The kingdom of God is always principal. And the kingdom of God is not of this world but is heavenly in origin. In other words, no human civil government has the responsibility to "usher in" the kingdom of God. Human government is subject to the authority of Jesus Christ and has a responsibility to Jesus Christ much like the individual has a responsibility to Jesus. Obviously, we are not talking about salvation; we are talking about the duty of obedience and laboring in this realm as a minister of the Lord.

The political arena is important because one of the duties of human government is to maintain an atmosphere favorable to the proclamation of the Gospel. Any human government that persecutes those who proclaim the truth of Christ as Lord and Savior is acting in a fashion contrary to its biblical mandate. At the same time, any human government that uses the sword to "convert" people to Christianity is likewise acting in a fashion contrary to the Bible. Civil government has the duty to restrain evil so the people of God might go about the business of bringing their individual spheres of influence under the authority of Jesus Christ. A civil government has very little responsibility beyond this duty of maintaining order in society. A man of Christ who has understanding will look at the current state of affairs and recognize our civil government has dramatically deviated from the biblical standard. In exceeding the proper bounds of civil government, our national, state and local civic leadership has forced Christians off of the playing field and have made it very difficult for Christians and Christian organizations to fulfill their obligations before God. In some ways it is easier for us to have a bloated civil government but that is not godly. It would be just as wrong for a wife to usurp her husband's role and force him to stand aside while she did what *he* was supposed to do.

It would be wrong to suggest the Bible demands a particular form of civil government although we do know from Scripture that any civil system should be limited so that individuals in free association have the opportunity to govern themselves under God. Civil government should not impose upon the individual or family to the extent that they are unable to fulfill their duty to God. It is not that the Bible requires a representative form of government: the Bible requires *limited* civil government.

We live in a nation that holds to a representative, republican form of government. Our founding fathers looked to traditional English freedoms, the best aspects of classical civil thought and to the Word of God when they fashioned the constitutional republic we live in today. However, the fact is, we do not live under the form of government they originally established. This is one of the things a man of Christ must understand in order to provide godly leadership in the political arena.

*Men Of Issachar*

## *Understand The Political Past*

The first thing Christian men must grasp in the realm of politics is the past. He must have a basic understanding of this nation's history. I'm not talking about the politically correct history students are force-fed in the public school. I am talking about the history of these United States according to the original documents. In other words, a man of Christ must have some familiarity with the world view that buttressed the birth of this nation.

A good place to start is with the constitutions of the original thirteen states. This is helpful because the state constitutions reveal the world view of colonial America even better than the U.S. Constitution. This is so because the state constitutions were closer to the common man, so to speak. Each state had numerous representatives in their individual state Congresses who contributed to the formation of these original thirteen governing documents. By the time the national Constitution was developed the field of representation had been narrowed considerably. Therefore, the original constitutions of the thirteen states tell us about the world view of the "entire" founding generation rather than limiting our understanding to the worldview of those who were participants in the Constitutional convention. Here is a *sampling* of what we find:

Delaware 1776 Constitution: ART. 22. "Every person who shall be chosen a member of either house, or appointed to any office or place of trust, before taking his seat, or entering upon the execution of his office, shall take the following oath, or affirmation, if conscientiously scrupulous of taking an oath, to wit: I, A. B., do profess faith in God the Father, and in Jesus Christ His only Son, and in the

Holy Ghost, one God, blessed for evermore; and I do acknowledge the holy scriptures of the Old and New Testament to be given by divine inspiration."

Georgia 1777 Constitution: ART. VI. "The representatives shall be chosen out of the residents in each county, who shall have resided at least twelve months in this state, and three months in the county where they shall be elected; except the freeholders of the counties of Glynn and Camden, who are in a state of alarm, and who shall have the liberty of choosing one member each, as specified in the articles of this constitution, in any other county, until they have residents sufficient to qualify them for more; and they shall be of the Protestant religion..."

Maryland 1776 Constitution: "That every person, appointed to any office of profit or trust, shall, before he enters on the execution thereof, take the following oath; to wit: "I, A. B., do swear, that I do not hold myself bound in allegiance to the King of Great Britain, and that I will be faithful, and bear true allegiance to the state of Maryland; and shall also subscribe a declaration of his belief in the Christian religion."

Massachusetts 1780 Constitution: Article I. "Any person chosen governor, lieutenant-governor, councillor, senator, or representative, and accepting the trust, shall, before he proceed to execute the duties of his place or office, make and subscribe the following declaration, viz: I, A.B., do declare that I believe the Christian religion, and have a firm persuasion of its truth; and that I am seized and possessed, in my own right, of the property required by the constitution, as one qualification for the office or place to which I am elected."

New Hampshire 1784 Constitution: "no person shall be capable of being elected a senator (representative or president), who is not of the Protestant religion"

New Jersey 1776 Constitution: "That there shall be no establishment of any one religious sect in this Province, in preference to another; and that no Protestant inhabitant of this Colony shall be denied the enjoyment of any civil right, merely on account of his religious principles; but that all persons, professing a belief in the faith of any Protestant sect, who shall demean themselves peaceably under the government, as hereby established, shall be capable of being elected into any office of profit or trust, or being a member of either branch of the Legislature, and shall fully and freely enjoy every privilege and immunity, enjoyed by others their fellow subjects."

North Carolina 1776 Constitution: "That no person, who shall deny the being of God or the truth of the Protestant religion, or the divine authority either of the Old or New Testaments, or who shall hold religious principles incompatible with the freedom and safety of the state, shall be capable of holding any office or place of trust or profit in the civil department within this state."

Pennsylvania 1776 Constitution: "And each member, before he takes his seat shall make and subscribe the following declaration, viz: I do believe in one God, the creator and governor of the universe, the rewarder of the good and the punisher of the wicked. And I do acknowledge the Scriptures of the Old and New Testament to be given by Divine inspiration. And no further or other religious test shall ever hereafter be required of any civil officer or magistrate in this state."

Virginia 1775 Declaration of Rights: "That

religion, or the duty which we owe to our Creator and the manner of discharging it, can be directed by reason and conviction, not by force or violence; and therefore, all men are equally entitled to the free exercise of religion, according to the dictates of conscience; and that it is the mutual duty of all to practice Christian forbearance, love, and charity towards each other."

Although Tennessee and Vermont were not among the original thirteen states, I've included excerpts from their original state constitutions for good measure.

Tennessee 1796 Constitution: "No person who denies the being of God or a future state of rewards and punishments, shall hold any office in the civil department of this state."

Vermont 1777 Constitution: "And each member, before he takes his seat, shall make and subscribe the following declaration, viz. 'I \_\_\_\_ do believe in one God, the Creator and Governor of the Diverse, the rewarder of the good and punisher of the wicked. And I do acknowledge the scriptures of the old and new testament to be given by divine inspiration, and own and profess the protestant religion.' And no further or other religious test shall ever, hereafter, be required of any civil officer or magistrate in this state."

Beyond a doubt the various bodies which came together to form the United States of America were Christian republics. What does this mean to the man of Christ? Are we to labor to return to days gone by? The answer is yes and no. I do not believe we should try to re-create every jot and tittle of colonial America. However, we *must* return to a worldview recognizing God as sovereign - in *every* human endeavor including politics. If we glean nothing else from these original state constitutions we must understand this nation was founded as a nation *under God*. It is unfortunate (and purposeful) that God is not mentioned in the national constitution. Thus, one of the things we need to do as men of Christ is to "reintroduce" God to the marketplace.

I want to make it clear that I am not saying the kingdom of God will be realized in this realm through the political process. My emphasis is on the fact that civil leaders have the duty to obey God and to rule according to the principles of Scripture. One of the first steps in the process of holding civil magistrates accountable to God's Word is to verify the fact that this nation was founded as a Christian commonwealth. A Christian nation in the sense that the laws of the land were based upon God's Word. A Christian nation in the sense that the people who served as civil leaders were supposed to have knowledge of God and his Word and acknowledge the exclusive truth of the Christian religion. Not a Christian nation in the sense that everyone is taxed to support the church or required to attend a particular church or whatever. None of that has a place in a Christian commonwealth. A Christian nation is simply a corporate people that acknowledges God as the sovereign ruler of the universe and understands there is no aspect of this life that is exempt from the authority of King Jesus. I should hasten to add, the only way there will ever be a return to our Christian roots is through evangelism and discipleship. Thus, men of Christ must approach this problem with a two-pronged attack. We will discuss what we ought to do later. At this point I simply want to make it clear that a man must understand the past if he hopes to be an effective leader in the present. The focus of this short book is on our duty to redeem our culture for Christ - including the arena of political action. Not because politics will solve our problems but because politics run amok will gum up the works and make it difficult for Christian individuals and Christian organizations to do the business they have been called to do.

## *Understand The Present*

Once we have a grip on the past we are then able to lead as men of Christ in the present - well almost. We must also have an *understanding* of the present. In other words, we need to be familiar with current events and able to judge them according to biblical standards. It is good to know this nation began as a Christian nation and that the worldview foundational to our country embraced the authority of God and his Word. It is also important to be able to look at what is going on around us and know how we deviate from our origins - and *why* we should return to the more elemental state of affairs.

I remind you that our thinking must be an expression of the mind of God. We must be immersed in the Word of God in order to think clearly about the world around us. As I've mentioned, Christian men have the ability to speak to every situation in life based on their familiarity with God's Word. Hence, when we study current affairs we must judge the data by the standard of the Bible.

The best way to understand the present time is through regular reading of the news and current books. Having said this I think you can understand why it is so important to view everything through the lens of God's Word. I'm not going to advocate any particular news organization at this point but if we know the Word we will be able to sift through the options available to us and discard those information sources that are pushing an agenda contrary to the Bible. And that is the key. We are not talking about any political party or even a particular political philosophy. I am not advocating any particular group but I *am* pushing a kingdom worldview. Since the man of God *can* judge all things he has the o*bligation* to gather information and to sift it.

The man of Christ should be able to read the news, read books, visit news sites on the internet and listen to informational radio with a discerning mind. It is not enough to say we ought to read conservative books or visit conservative news sites. We must sift everything and judge everything by the standard of God's Word. We are not supposed to be lackeys for any particular political organization; we are supposed to be citizens of the kingdom of heaven.

There are a number of books I might recommend but I caution you against the human tendency to wrap a particular political philosophy in the robe of Christianity and consider it a settled issue. The truth is we have not seen godly government in this nation for many generations. Some political leaders have been better than others but the trend in our national, state, and even local civil governments has been toward a humanistic political philosophy. In other words, the trend has been to remove God from the throne and put (corporate) man in his place.

Our goal is to understand the political philosophy that gives energy to this trend. Moreover, we need to familiarize ourselves with the tactics of those who hope to establish utopia by means of power religion. Realize there is a conspiracy afoot. It is not a conspiracy in the sense of something hidden; it is an open conspiracy that began in the Garden of Eden. It is an attempt to make man the measure of all things. It is the attempt to secure salvation through law and by force. This is what humanistic, godless government is all about. The man of Christ must understand the inner workings of power religion and know how it differs from the kingdom of God. In a nutshell humanistic government is about force. The kingdom of God is about faith.

Men need to be keen students of current affairs and practical theologians able to gather information and sift data, judging it according to the Word of God. Once that has been accomplished, men of Christ must articulate a theology of family, church and civil governance that is in compliance with God's Word. Finally, men must develop the practical steps necessary to implement godly government. This is leadership that understands present times.

### *Understand The Future*

Men of Christ must also understand the future. There are two aspects to this. On the one hand, men should realize what will happen if nothing is done about the current situation. This means we infer the past and the present and are able to produce a reasonable prediction of where we will eventually end if nothing is done. On the other hand, men should be able to formulate a picture of what we can expect if we acknowledge the sovereignty of God in all areas of life. Obviously no one can do this with 100% accuracy. Yet, if a man of Christ has understanding he will be able to speak intelligently about the future.

*Men Of Issachar*

Most important, however, is the understanding of God's plan for this world. In his letter to the church in Colosse Paul says, *For by Him all things were created that are in heaven and that are on earth, visible and invisible, whether thrones or dominions or principalities or powers. All things were created through Him and for Him. And He is before all things, and in Him all things consist. And He is the head of the body, the church, who is the beginning, the firstborn from the dead, that in all things He may have the preeminence. For it pleased the Father that in Him all the fullness should dwell, and by Him to reconcile all things to Himself, by Him, whether things on earth or things in heaven, having made peace through the blood of His cross* (Colossians 1:16-20). In other words, Christ is the head of the church so that he might be the head of all things. He is the head of his redeemed people so that he might redeem all of creation. All creation is reconciled to God through Jesus Christ as each member of his body brings their arena of activity under Christ's authority. Men of Christ must understand this future if they hope to lead in the present. They must understand that God's will shall not be thwarted. The gospel of Jesus Christ *will* be victorious. Not every human being on the face of the earth will embrace Jesus Christ as Lord and Savior. There will always be "salt marshes" which are not healed by the waters of the gospel (Ezekiel 47:11). Nevertheless, all lawful and legitimate human endeavors are to be brought under the lordship of Jesus that he might be glorified and have preeminence in every aspect of this life and realm. If we hope to lead as God would have us lead, we need to understand this basic fact.

## Conclusion: Understand Leadership

Godly leadership is always servant leadership; men of Christ must lead as Jesus does. In addition, they must hold other leaders accountable to the same standard. In every way, Christian men must lead by example.

Previously I said men *always* lead whether they want to or not. They may lead in the wrong direction and so lead their family and others into confusion. They may lead in a self-centered fashion and thereby lead those under their care into a similar lifestyle. But because men have been designed to lead they cannot get away from the responsibility of leadership.

Thus, men of Christ *must* be servant leaders. They must be willing to lay their life down in order to lead. This is *the* critical issue a man must grasp. He must realize he leads whether he wants to or not and if he is going to lead in a godly way he must lead through an example of self-sacrifice. He must understand that the needs of his wife and children come before those of his own. He must understand that he is required to step out of his comfort zone in order to shoulder leadership as he should. He must understand that servant leadership is the rule no matter where he might exercise authority. Self sacrificial servant leadership is required in the family, the church and the civil realm. This self sacrificing, servant leadership is the way men bring their field of duty under the authority of Jesus Christ; it is how men lead those under their care into a deeper understanding of Christ and his kingdom.

People learn primarily by watching someone else. Men must understand they lead best when imitating Jesus.

*Men Of Issachar*

Men of Christ, I encourage you to understand the Bible, God and yourself. I encourage you to understand the times. I encourage you to lead.

# Chapter 5
## Know What To Do

*For I have known him, in order that he may command his children and his household after him, that they keep the way of the LORD, to do righteousness and justice, that the LORD may bring to Abraham what He has spoken to him* (Genesis 18:19).

I made the claim that the solution to our current cultural crisis is found when men of Christ live in obedience to the Lord Jesus. It is my contention we can solve the problems we face in the family, the church and the civil realm through the leadership of Christian men. I stated that men of Christ must understand the times and know what to do.

We need to realize this is not a "natural" outcome, as if the solution to the world's problems lie in the efforts of man. Instead, it is essential to recognize the benefits we receive when men lead is a consequence of God blessing his followers for their obedience. Even then the blessing and the "success" may not match up with our expectations. If our definition of success is worldly, we will be disappointed because God understands success as growth in

*Men Of Issachar*

Christlikeness.

Although the kingdom of God is realized as men of Christ bring their arena of responsibility under the authority of the Lord Jesus, the profound blessing of worldwide impact is likely many years in the future. Today, Christian men are to do the work of laying a foundation. We must be like the men who worked to build the soaring cathedrals of medieval times. Hundreds, perhaps thousands, of workers were involved in the construction of those magnificent places of worship and many of them did not live to see them completed. However, each man worked at what he was called to do and produced that part of the cathedral he was assigned. In other words, the men who worked to build those impressive structures were responsible for their do-main of activity and it was only because they did the job they were called to do that the cathedral was eventually finished.

So our leadership must be leadership of a most unselfish kind. It is leadership designed to lay a foundation for the future. It is leadership designed to bring others to their fullest potential. It is leadership of service - not for our own glory but for the glory of God and the benefit of others. It is service that will lay the groundwork for the bearing of fruit in the future.

This does not mean we will not benefit in our own experience. We will benefit in many ways! As we bring our sphere of influence under the authority of Jesus through Christlike servant leadership, we will begin to see the blessings of the messianic kingdom realized in our own domain.

Ultimately, we must do what we do for the sake of Christ, our King, our captain, our friend and our brother. There is joy in a job well done and it is my aim to show you how you might experience that joy by knowing what to do as an individual, as a leader in your family, as a leader in the church and in the community.

## Individual: Thoughts

The first area where men of Christ must know what to do is in their personal lives. The first person a man of Christ must learn to lead is himself and we do that by following the example of Jesus. This means we live in obedience to the Holy Bible. In short, we must learn to walk as Jesus walked. This concerns our thought life, what we say and what we do.

Many men believe their thought life is no one's business but their own. They think they can entertain sinful thoughts as long as they don't act upon those ideas. They believe as long as they keep their fantasies to themselves it doesn't matter what they think because it won't affect the "real world." The Bible teaches otherwise. And with most men, the secret thoughts they cherish have to do with sex.

Jesus said to look upon a woman with lust is to commit adultery with her. Obviously, that doesn't mean it is exactly the same as the physical act. But it does mean that what men think is important. A man may not act upon his lustful thoughts but he would be a fool to believe those lustful thoughts (or murderous thoughts or envious thoughts and so on), do not have an effect upon his behavior.

A man who entertains sexual fantasies will treat his wife improperly. Either he will push her to fulfill his x-rated expectations or he will deal with her in a loveless fashion because she does not measure up to his fantasy. Morally we are of a single piece.

Sexual fantasy will reveal itself in a dissatisfaction with your wife and that will be manifest in your lack of love for her. You will not want to serve her and to respect her. You will not want to give yourself up for her because, after all, she isn't as exciting as the fantasy.

The life of a man of Christ must be undergirded by righteous thoughts. I mention the problem of sexual fantasy because it is common with men. Unfortunately, I have talked with men (including other pastors) who think sexual fantasy is no big deal as long as it "doesn't get in the way" of their marriage relationship. Believe me, it will always get in the way of your marriage relationship.

Therefore, the first place a man of Christ must lead himself is in his thought life. He must be sure his mind is on *whatever is true, whatever is honorable, whatever is just, whatever is pure, whatever is lovely, whatever is commendable, if there is any excellence, if there is anything worthy of praise, think about these things* (Philippians 4:8). In short, our thought life must be as presentable as our physical life. We cannot fool ourselves into thinking it is okay to live a dual life. It is not.

The man of Christ must spend time cultivating godly thought. He must read the Bible and meditate upon its precepts. He must discipline himself to turn away from things that lead his thoughts astray: turn off the TV, put down the trashy magazine, toss out the raunchy books. Get rid of whatever it is that leads your thoughts astray. Again, I use the example of lust because it is the most common problem men face but you know yourself well enough to identify those additional things *you* ought to avoid.

*Know What To Do*

## *Individual: Actions*

A sanctified thought life gives birth to a Christlike example in our day to day living. This is where the imitation of Jesus Christ is most readily expressed. Many people ask me how they can learn to live in a Christlike fashion. Many times men will come to me and say they just can't seem to do what they ought to do. They tell me they don't want to "fake it" and so find they are unable to make progress in cultivating a life that is pleasing to the Lord Jesus. What they must realize is that we learn to live righteously through imitation. As the apostle Paul said to the church in Ephesus, *Therefore be imitators of God, as beloved children. And walk in love, as Christ loved us and gave himself up for us, a fragrant offering and sacrifice to God* (Ephesians 5:1-2). We learn to walk as Jesus walked by imitating the examples of the Father and the Son.

We learn to do what is right in the same way a child learns to walk and talk. A child sees how it is done and does his best to copy it. In a sense, a Christlike life begins with playacting. Of course it doesn't stop there; playacting must become who we really are. It is simply a matter of cultivating the new creation. But in the beginning of our Christian walk it may seem forced and even hypocritical. Yet, we should not feel that way any more than a child who is attempting to imitate his natural father would feel hypocritical because what he attempts to imitate does not come naturally. This is how children learn. Little girls learn to be mothers by playing with dolls and playing house. Little boys learn to be men and to be fathers by watching daddy and carrying their briefcase to the door with daddy as he goes to work.

I remember my sons imitating me when they

*Men Of Issachar*

were little. My wife once told me that our oldest boy was proud that he was able to preach "long sermons" from only a few verses in the Bible. Apparently he would occasionally gather his brothers and sisters (along with a few stuffed toys to fill the "pews") and preach sermons to them - in imitation of his daddy. This is the way children learn. They don't really know much about what they are imitating but they do know they want to be like their dad or their mom. We should have the same attitude. Indeed, *unless you are converted and become as little children, you will by no means enter the kingdom of heaven* (Matthew 18:3). Unless we are willing to play copy-cat we will not come under the authority of the Messiah.

    The passage I quoted earlier from Ephesians tells us we should be imitators of God, like dear children. We should also be imitators of Jesus Christ much as a younger sibling might imitate an older brother or perhaps a favorite uncle. The fact is we can do both when we look to Jesus Christ as our example. In John chapter 14 we are told that Phillip said to Jesus, *"Lord, show us the Father, and it is enough for us."* Jesus replied, *"Have I been with you so long, and you still do not know me, Philip? Whoever has seen me has seen the Father. How can you say, 'Show us the Father'?"* (John 14:8-9). Therefore if we wish to imitate our father in heaven and imitate the firstborn among many brethren (our older brother) we need to examine the life of Jesus Christ and strive to walk as he walked (1 John 2:6).

    Understand, the only other choice we have is to imitate the Devil. The apostle John said our behavior manifests who we are. He said, *in this the children of God and the children of the devil are manifest: whoever does not practice righteousness*

*Know What To Do*

*is not of God, nor is he who does not love his brother* (1 John 3:10). John merely echoes Jesus who told the Jews who rejected him that they were like their father the devil and the desires of their father is what they wanted to do. Jesus said the devil *was a murderer from the beginning, and has nothing to do with the truth, because there is no truth in him. When he lies, he speaks out of his own character, for he is a liar and the Father of lies* (John 8:44). No man of Christ wants to imitate the devil or to be confused with a child of the devil. This is why it is so important for us to get past this dumb idea that it is hypocritical to imitate, to copy, to playact and to try to be like Jesus even if we don't "feel like it." If we *do* it, we *become* it; imitation is simply "assembling" the new creation that we already are in Christ.

We cannot limit ourselves to the Gospels in our effort to know Jesus in order to imitate him. Christ is displayed on every page of Scripture. There are examples in Scripture of how we should act examples of how we should *not* act. There is wisdom literature telling us how the Lord thinks and prophecy explaining what he does and why he does it. There is law, poetry, epic tales and so on - all designed to present us with the character of the Trinity so we might imitate our Lord and Savior – and we must imitate him in thought, word and action.

A primary character quality we ought to imitate is the humility of Jesus Christ. The Bible makes it very clear that Jesus is humble. This doesn't mean he is weak; it means he knows his duty and "knows his place." Even within the Trinity there is subordination. Jesus, the Eternal Son who had taken human flesh upon himself, did not do his own will but the will of the Father. Jesus knew what it meant to be under authority. And this humility is best displayed in Christ's willingness to sacrifice himself for his Bride. Men find it easy to be "servant leaders" when they receive praise for their "selfless" behavior. Yet, all too often, the big man at church - the humble willing servant at church - is a tyrant at home. Obviously this has no relationship to the kind of leadership Jesus Christ provides his Bride. Thus, our Christlike leadership is put to the test first at home.

    Practically speaking, a man of Christ will always consider what is best for the other person, even at great cost to himself. This takes wisdom. It requires a man to imitate God in his thoughts. He must consider whether his actions will help the other person become more like Jesus Christ or if they will confirm the other in some sin. For example, it may seem the most Christlike action would be to encourage your wife to get involved in extra church activities even though she is already stretched too thin at home. It is good to serve others but only as God equips. Many times my wife has thanked me for guiding her away from taking on a particular obligation outside the home. It has allowed her to focus her energy where her heart is - and my decision provided her an inviolable reason for turning down the "opportunity" to serve on yet another committee.

### *Family*

    I suspect many women are married to men who act like angels at church but are devils at home. These women long for a true man of Christ to protect and lead them. In his letter to the church at Ephesus Paul wrote, *Wives, submit to your own husbands, as to the Lord. For the husband is the head of the wife even as Christ is the head of the church, his body, and is himself its Savior. Now as the church submits to Christ, so also wives should submit in everything to their husbands. Husbands, love your wives, as Christ loved the church and gave himself up for her, that he might sanctify her, having cleansed her by the washing of water with the word, so that he might present the church to himself in splendor, without spot or wrinkle or any such thing, that she might be holy and without blemish. In the same way husbands should love their wives as their own bodies. He who loves his wife loves himself. For no one ever hated his own flesh, but nourishes and cherishes it, just as Christ does the church, because we are members of his body. "Therefore a man shall leave his Father and mother and hold fast to his wife, and the two shall become one flesh." This mystery is profound, and I am saying that it refers to Christ and the church. However, let each one of you love his wife as himself, and let the wife see that she respects her husband* (Ephesians 5:22-33).

Men like to emphasize the first portion which says wives must submit to their husbands as to the Lord. However, when it comes to the man's responsibility, they find excuses for their failure to obey the plain words of Scripture. Many men say, "I *would* treat my wife like Christ treats the church if she would only submit to me." This is a lame excuse. Nowhere does the Bible say a man can forgo his responsibility to act in a Christlike fashion toward his wife if she refuses to uphold her end of the deal. The truth is, there is mutual submission within the marriage relationship. But it is also true that the man has an obligation to lead. He must step out first

*Men Of Issachar*

and serve in order to model the behavior his wife (and children) should follow.

Paul showed the way when he told the church at Corinth that they should imitate him even as he imitates Jesus Christ (1 Corinthians 11:1). Each of us should be able to tell our wife and children they can imitate us because we imitate Jesus Christ. This is the heart of servant leadership.

Servant leadership does not mean you are a slave to every whim of your spouse. It means you will do what is best for her and wisely guide her into greater conformity to God's Word.

Servant leadership also means you are willing to set aside your own desire in order to become the man you should be for your wife and children to imitate. It means you think of others more highly than yourself. It means you study the Bible so you can teach your family the things of God even when you would rather read the newspaper or watch the ball game on TV. It means you set the vision and direction for your family and articulate to them what it is God asks of his people, explaining to your wife and children how they can participate in the reconciliation of creation back to the Creator (Colossians 1:20).

As a servant leader, you blaze the trail for your family. You study the Bible, you develop a prayer life, you work at your job as unto the Lord, you find ways to help out around the house even when you are tired from a long day's work, you give an encouraging word and godly advice tailored to the needs of each person in your family. This is servant leadership. It is laying down your life for the sake of others. It doesn't mean you abandon your own calling or your hopes and dreams. It means you look to the resources God has given you in your wife and children and develop those resources so the vision God has placed upon your heart and the calling he has given you will be fulfilled according to his desire.

God has given each man of Christ the wife and family he needs to fulfill the calling on his life. The irony is that the calling on his life will only be fulfilled as he brings his wife and children to their fullest potential. That's what it means to husband a woman. It means to nurture her so she will be everything God intended for her to be and in so doing, she will be the woman *you* need in order to achieve what God has placed upon your heart. This is the paradox in the family relationship. Men must give of themselves in order to be blessed in their calling. Men must lay their life down so they can build up the life and ministry of another and as a result they enrich their own life and ministry. In short, when a man focuses on service to his wife and children, the fulfillment of his calling will follow.

This is what Jesus did. He laid his life down so his Bride could experience the fullness of relationship with the Creator. He laid his life down and suffered so his Bride might be cleansed and made clean. Jesus died so his Bride may participate in the process of taking dominion over creation for the glory of God and the benefit of mankind.

The husband is the head of the wife as Christ is head of the church because he brings her into a place of salvation. I don't mean he saves her soul from hell. I mean that through his servant leadership the wife (and the children in turn) will experience God's salvation in her arena of activity. Part of the problem is that we don't understand what salvation means. We think it has to do with the

*Men Of Issachar*

saving of one's soul from hell. That is only part of it. Salvation is comprehensive. In other words, *all* of creation is redeemed through the salvific work of Jesus Christ because salvation is about redemption and reconciliation. Paul says we have been given a ministry of reconciliation meaning we are tools in God's hand to bring our field of responsibility back into relationship with the Creator. We are instruments of God used to bring our sphere of influence under the authority of Jesus Christ so we may give praise to him through the part of creation for which we are responsible. And the primary field of responsibility for a married man of Christ is his family.

A husband's job (in part) is to convey his wife and children to a place where they are able to bring their sphere of influence under the authority of Jesus and reconcile that part of creation to the Creator. A husband is to be an instrument in the hand of God enabling his wife to succeed in her task of dominion and reconciliation. As she does so she will contribute to the fulfillment of the calling God has placed upon her husband. This is what it means for the two to be one. This is why it is important for a man to marry a woman who is right for him and can contribute to that vision and calling of God. In other words, her calling must match his calling and enhance it.

A husband has the responsibility to sanctify and cleanse and wash his wife with the Word in words and deeds. This is not a cleansing from sin and or justification before God but a cleansing through leadership. A man must be a good example and lovingly direct his wife and children along the path of Christlike behavior. This responsibility is often abused by men; that means the man is not first

*Know What To Do*

leading himself down the path of righteousness. This is where church leadership comes into play. If a man is abusive and judgmental, the wife has the right - indeed the duty - to bring the problem to the attention of church leadership. She has a duty because if she loves her husband, she will want to see him do what is right. If her example of Christ-likeness is not enough to steer him true, she will need help from the church.

Furthermore, a man makes his wife presentable to Christ in the coming together of man and wife in ministry (again, we are not talking about justification). The wife is presentable if the husband is presentable. Think about it; Christ loved the church and gave himself for her in order to sanctify her and cleanse her so that he might present her to himself a glorious church. If Jesus had not done what he was supposed to do, if he had not been the servant leader he was supposed to be, then his Bride would not have been without spot and blemish. Therefore, we know one way a woman is presentable to Christ is when her husband is likewise presentable to Christ. She is fulfilled in her ministry and expressing Jesus in her sphere of influence as she ought, when her husband is fulfilling his duty and is expressing Christ to his sphere of influence as he ought. In this way a man and a woman both submit to their individual duties before the Lord and are blessed as they bless one another.

This is not to say a man or woman is presentable to Jesus only if he or she is married. It does recognize that a married person has the responsibility to fulfill the duties of the marriage covenant. Once married, a person is beholden to God for the stipulations of the covenant arrangement. He cannot

*Men Of Issachar*

do whatever he wants. Both man and wife must conform to God's will *as a married couple*. In many ways, the rules are different for a married man or woman than for a single person. If a you find this unacceptable, you should not get married.

So we have seen that a man leads through self-sacrifice as he serves his wife so she may blossom into the woman God intends. Thus, the goal of a man of Christ must be to nurture and care of those under his authority. His job is to maximize the potential of his followers. Just as Paul found his reward in doing the work of a pastor, a man must find his reward in doing all he can to bring his wife and children into the kingdom of God. This is how we measure a man's success. This is why a man must be a leader at home before he can be a leader in the church.

I am not suggesting a man has the privilege of neglecting his own gifts. What I am saying is that his gifts and calling are enhanced as his wife dovetails with him and they do the work of the kingdom together.

A Christian man must lead in the family situation by providing a good example and by actively teaching God's ways to his wife, children and grandchildren. In so doing, a man is expressing true Christlike leadership. Failure to do this does not mean a man ceases to lead; it merely means he will lead poorly.

The family is the basic building block of society and societal change must begin with the family. Familial change begins with the husband leading and loving his wife, just as Christ leads and loves the church. And the successful experience of leading at home enables a man to lead at church.

## *Church*

We have already covered the topic of male leadership in the church so now we need to discuss what men of Christ should *do* as leaders in the church.

To begin with, Christian men must continue to imitate the Lord so others within their sphere of influence will have a good example to imitate. When there are godly men in the church, there are good examples for people to follow. New believers benefit from having a real life illustration to help them learn how to walk as Jesus walked. Therefore, the first thing men of Christ do as leaders in the church is model Christlikeness.

Yet when we talk in specific terms about leadership in the church, one of the first things we note is that the church leaders should prayerfully determine the mission or vision for the local body. Every expression of Christ's body needs to develop a mission statement explaining how they will bring salvation in Christ to bear in their arena of activity. Each gathering of Believers should have a vision of how they can serve their community as an expression of those under Christ's lordship. Every Believer is called to go into all the world with the gospel but every church will have different gifts represented in the Body, so each local fellowship will fulfill the Great Commission in a different way. This is the vision determined by the leaders of the church.

Church leaders will arrive at this mission statement in a variety of ways. In a new church or plant, the leadership will establish a church, which from its inception, has a particular goal in mind. For instance, a church plant would typically have evangelism as a primary goal. Therefore, as the leadership team assembles a core group they will look for men and families who are gifted in ways that support that vision.

An established church may determine its mission to the community by considering who God has brought to their fellowship. In any case, men lead in the church by establishing the vision for that church and deciding how that particular company can best work out its ministry of reconciliation.

Men continue to lead by putting feet to the vision: they must do more than merely articulate what that local body is about (and there may be several aspects to the church's mission). They must also take the lead in getting it done. So a church focused on serving the community through educational outreach must have men in leadership who are willing and able to lead by example. Men in the body must be willing to organize a Christian school and teach or give administrative oversight. If the church vision includes reaching out to families in financial need then the men of the church must be prepared to lead by providing financial counseling and over-sight to those who teach housekeeping skills, shopping skills and so on. No matter what the vision or the mission of the church, men need to take the lead by *doing* that ministry in the community.

Church leadership should also maximize the potential of the flock. Just as a father should identify the gifting God has given to each member of his household, church leadership ought to identify the talent within their own fellowship. This is not to say church leaders should "lay down the law" about what a person can or cannot do in service but church leaders should hone their godly thinking skills in order to provide sound advice and direction in helping the flock do the work of the kingdom.

When church leaders serve the Body in this fashion they are not doing so in order to receive anything from the church. Leaders must serve self sacrificially. Normally there will be paid staff members but when I talk about church leadership I'm talking about men in the church who serve as elders and deacons and have as their calling the oversight of the flock. These men have the job of nurturing the church so if the senior pastor moves on, the church will not fall apart. If the leadership does its job properly, things will not go to pieces when one (or more) leader leaves. The flock should not look to a human leader for stability but to the great Shepherd of the sheep, Jesus Christ.

The job of the church leader is to help each individual member of the body grow in their relationship with Jesus Christ and to help them bring their arena of activity under his lordship. Primarily this will be a ministry to the heads of households. There will be times when church leaders need to address an issue in a family but normally their job is to help the heads of households shepherd their own flock at home.

When men exercise Christlike leader-ship, others shine. When men do not lead or "lead" selfishly, others suffer. When men try to be first according to the world's way of exercising leadership, they end up last and those they are called to lead are shortchanged. This is true in the family, the church - and the community.

### *Community*

Men are not supposed to drop the idea of servant leadership when they lead in the community. God's way of doing things is not limited to a narrow slice of reality but is applicable to every aspect of life. Obviously, we will not do exactly the same things in the community that we would do in the family or in the church, but the basis of leadership remains the same. Therefore, men must lead in the community as servant leaders expressing the character of Jesus Christ just as they would express Christ anywhere else.

Community leadership is not limited to public office. A man of Christ can lead in his community as a business owner who runs his shop in a way that is pleasing to his Lord and Savior. This, of course, requires an understanding of what a godly business looks like. Hence, a man of Christ who wants to express leadership in his community through his business needs to know the Bible and how to apply the principles he finds there to his particular occupation.

Godly business owners should also be involved in the local Chamber of Commerce and other community organizations that allow them to serve their fellow citizens as God brings opportunity. This will enable him to serve as an example to other business owners as well.

A man of Christ need not be a business owner to express the kingdom to his community. He can serve through something as simple as a letter to the editor. He can serve as a member of a local civic organization. He can serve his community by being a good employee and looking for opportunities to make his employer successful so the firm he works for may be a blessing to his neighbors.

A Christian man must know his talents and abilities in order to use those God-given gifts to serve in his community in an effective way. It will do little

*Know What To Do*

good for a man to serve in the civic realm in a way that does not match what God has made him to be. Not everyone should seek public office. Not everyone should apply for a job in law enforcement. Not every man of Christ needs to join a community service club. So, men need to know what God has designed them to do in the public square.

Recognize that your arena of activity may be quite limited. You might think an ability to write (for instance) is wasted unless you publish a bestseller. That isn't the case. God may want you to write a weekly letter to the editor concerning hometown issues that need to be addressed from a biblical point of view. He may want you to use your spectacular singing voice to participate in a community choir or in singing the national anthem at local events. The Lord might want you to use your persuasive public speaking ability in attending city council meetings and presenting your (biblically based) case as a private citizen. The point is, we cannot fall into the trap of thinking as the world thinks. God does not necessarily give unique talent and ability to a man so he can become rich and famous. We should not be disappointed with the limited reach of our service. God is the one who opens the doors and God calls us to serve where we are at. There is nothing wrong with expanding our arena of activity but that should not be our primary goal. Our job is to serve in the place God has put us, not to build our own little kingdom.

Also, be careful to serve in a godly fashion. This should be obvious but sometimes we are tempted to "baptize" worldly methods in order to get something done. For instance, our service to the community may be in working to roll back overreach

*Men Of Issachar*

on the part of City Hall. Even if we are trying to amend something the civil government has enacted we cannot make use of ungodly tactics. For instance, a favorite tactic of leftist radicals is to use ridicule as a weapon. The idea is to belittle civic representatives and make them look like fools so they will be more inclined to listen to the "little man" (cf. Paul Alinsky, *Rules For Radicals)*. It should be obvious this is ungodly. In fact, if you read the books recommending this behavior it becomes clear the strategy is satanic in origin. Men of Christ cannot abandon godliness at any point. We must be servant leaders at home, in the church and in the community as well.

### *Conclusion*

I suppose a man might say, "these are troubled times" no matter what age he lives in. Christians in the first century lived in troubled times and were severely persecuted for their faith. Indeed, the first few centuries of the New Testament era were years of hardship and tribulation for the people of God. Throughout history there have been many times of trouble for Believers.

Yet we are living at this time and age and it *is* true that these are troubled times. It is also true that no matter what happens, God is the sovereign ruler of the universe. Thus, as men of Christ began to understand the times and do what they ought, the success of their venture should not to be measured by worldly standards.

The work you do for the kingdom of God may never reach beyond your own backyard. If that is the arena of activity to which God has called you, then exercise servant leadership in *that* sphere of influence with everything you've got. Everything we do, we must do heartily as unto the Lord and under-

*Know What To Do*

stand it has great meaning and purpose - whether or not the world agrees.

Doing what a man of Christ should do will always be of value in the kingdom. It has value because it pleases our Lord and Savior, because it lays the foundation for our activity in eternity and because it is an expression of our love for God. I encourage you to be a man of Christ, to understand the times and do what you ought to do.

# CHAPTER 6
## KINGDOM PRACTICALITIES

This chapter will enlarge on the previous section and outline a man's individual, family, church and community practicalities in light of Christ's Lordship. In other words, we will talk about how you can make practical application of the theology we have discussed thus far.

***Individual Practicalities***

As a man of Christ the first thing you must do is settle the issue in your own mind: whom will you serve? You can serve the Lord God, ruler of heaven and earth or you can serve your puny little self. It is amazing that this is a difficult choice for most of us. Nonetheless, it is a very real choice. Thus, you must *choose you this day whom ye will serve* (Joshua 24:15, KJV).

Once you have decided to serve God you need to commit yourself to cultivating the new creation. Do not forget that the gift of salvation given you in Jesus Christ requires some assembly. Therefore, you need to develop a Bible reading regimen (I recommend the Bible reading schedule mentioned in chapter four) and a robust prayer life. You do these things in imitation of Jesus Christ. Obviously, Jesus

## Kingdom Practicalities

knew the word of God (he was the word made flesh) and spent plenty of time in prayer. You need to imitate him in these disciplines. It might feel "phony" in the beginning because it goes against the impression left behind by the old man. However, that sense of phoniness will fade as you buckle down and do what a man of God should do. If it does *not* start to fade, you need to backup a step and examine yourself to see if you are really in the faith (2 Corinthians 13:5).

I recommend you use a prayer list when you are in communication with your heavenly Father. Your list should reflect the outline of prayer given us by the Lord Jesus. This outline covers the five points of the covenant sequence (see, Meredith Kline, *The Structure Of Biblical Authority* and Ray Sutton, *That You May Prosper*) Therefore, it is an outline for prayer *and* for living.

The outline Jesus provided for the individual says, *Our Father in heaven, Hallowed be Your name. Your kingdom come. Your will be done On earth as it is in heaven. Give us day by day our daily bread. And forgive us our sins, For we also forgive everyone who is indebted to us. And do not lead us into temptation, But deliver us from the evil one* (Luke 11:2-4). The example given in Matthew is intended for corporate prayer and so ends with a doxology.

In this prayer we acknowledge that God is sovereign; that he has a hierarchy of order and has provided representation for us in Jesus Christ; that he expects us to obey his law; that he blesses his people and that he has provided for the continuity of his covenant. The breakdown looks like this:

1. Sovereignty: *Our Father in heaven, Hallowed be Your name.*

2. Hierarchy/Representation: *Your kingdom come.*
3. Law/Ethics: *Your will be done On earth as it is in heaven.*
4. Blessing/Sanctions: *Give us day by day our daily bread. And forgive us our sins, For we also forgive everyone who is indebted to us.*
5. Continuity: *And do not lead us into temptation, But deliver us from the evil one.*

    If you hope to pray aright, you need to pray with intelligence and purpose; you are more likely to do so when you follow this outline, in imitation of Jesus Christ.

    As you grow closer to the Lord through reading, studying and meditating on his word and through a vibrant prayer life, you will become more aware of situations in your life that need attention. If you are sensitive to the Holy Spirit you will find you can no longer overlook these things and will need to ask the Lord to give you the desire and the ability to deal violently with your besetting sins. Since I am writing to men I can say without equivocation that one of the besetting sins you deal with is lust. I think it was Philip Yancey who said he was disappointed to find marriage didn't solve the lust problem. He's right. And it's time men of Christ admit as much.

    You need to get rid of everything in your life that leads you into sexual sin. If you've seen the movie "Fireproof" you will recall the scene where Caleb Holt (Kirk Cameron's character) smashes his computer and throws it away. If that's what it takes, then do it.

    That is the sort of commitment to purity you need in order to move forward in the kingdom of God. You are called to imitate Jesus Christ because *you* are to be someone others can look to and

## Kingdom Practicalities

imitate. You may not realize that you will be imitated whether you're a good example or not. Moreover, those under your authority will imitate even those aspects of your life you think are secret. This is a spiritual principal you cannot escape. "Dear children" always imitate their Father even if it is "subconsciously." For instance, if you are nurturing illicit sexual desire by surfing porno sites on the internet you can be sure your children - both boys and girls – will likewise have problems with sexual deviancy. I'm not suggesting they're going to turn into animalistic sexual perverts. I *am* telling you they will experience a greater struggle with sexual temptation than they otherwise would, along with a heavier burden of self loathing and shame that accompanies it, especially in young people. Secret sexual sin is not the only thing they will imitate. Any unlawful thought or act you willfully cultivate - openly or in secret - is going to show up in the lives of those who are under your care. Believe me when I say this is true; I've learned it the hard way.

So, discipline yourself. Know the character of God and his Eternal Son like the back of your hand so you can imitate the Lord and thus be worthy of imitation. Live your Christian life moment by moment. Seek constant communication with the Lord and live a mindful Christian life rather than just drifting along with the flow of events.

Finally, develop the gifts God has given you. You were born with certain natural gifts and reborn with additional gifts given by the Holy Spirit. A man of Christ must discern these gifts – both natural and spiritual – and maximize them for the sake of the kingdom. Then he must put them to work in a lifelong effort to manifest the authority of Jesus Christ

*Men Of Issachar*

in his life and sphere of influence.
### *Family Practicalities*
The most important thing you can do for your family is to have a right relationship with the Lord Jesus Christ. The second most important thing you can do is to have a right relationship with your wife. If you want a peaceful, stable household you will imitate the Lord and lay down your life for your bride. Your wife must be the most cherished person in your life. She must be your most trusted friend and adviser. She must be the undisputed manager of the home. This does not mean she will "wear the pants in the family" but that you and the rest of the family will recognize her position as the manager of the household. I think it was Douglas Wilson who said a man should consider himself an honored guest in his own home, respecting the management of the household his wife provides and insisting the children do the same (by the way, here's your first reading assignment: Doug Wilson's book *Reforming Marriage*).

A Christian man also has the responsibility to teach his household. You need to know the Word so you can conduct a daily Bible study with your wife and children. It has been my practice over the years to work through one book of the Bible at a time. We usually study a few verses (or more) each evening and then have family prayer. Normally we "pray around the room" so every member of the family has an opportunity to pray. At our house we always conclude with my wife's prayer and then my own.

In order to teach, you need to be taught. Be sure you are reading the Bible and solid books on a variety of topics. Start with the "Worldview Reading List" in the addendum. Make sure you attend to the preaching at your church. Discuss the sermon with your family each Sunday evening.

Along these same lines, it is critical for you to be intimately involved in the education of your children. It won't do you any good to "lead" your family if you turn your children over to the anti-God public school system. Don't kid yourself: unless you are willing to break with the past on this issue of education ("it was good enough for me") you can expect limited success in leading your family to the "next level" of discipleship. At the very least you should have your children attend a good Christian school. However, it is best to educate them at home. I'm not going to go into detail about how to home school (there are plenty of resources that will instruct you in how to be a home educator) but will simply say it is imperative for Christians to make a break with the status quo when it comes to education. All education is religious. If you would refuse to have your children attend the local LDS religious edifice to learn about the kingdom of God then why in the world are you willing to let them be indoctrinated in an equally godless system five days a week, six or seven hours a day? Clearly, you should not be.

One caveat: homeschooling is not a cure-all. If you educate your children at home but rule your household like a tyrant you will end up doing more damage to your family than if you were to send your children to the public institution and properly nurture them the rest of the time. Attending the public school and coming home to a loving, godly father would be better than home schooling under the headship of a despot. Sure, public school kids *always* end up with a convoluted worldview and *always* find it difficult to understand kingdom reality thereafter. But that's better than being crippled by emotional abuse at the hands of the one who is supposed to guide and protect. Don't get me wrong; I'm not trying to set up a relativistic false dilemma. I'm simply trying to convey to you how important it is to be a loving father. There is nothing that can take the place of that in a child's life.

As a man of God you must also model manly devotion to your work. Do your job heartily as unto the Lord. This includes avoiding the nightly gripe session when you get home from work - as an employee or a business owner.

While we are on the subject, I recommend that every man have his own business. It may not be your sole source of income but if there is any way you can use the gifts God has given you to exercise your entrepreneurial muscle, I highly recommend it. It will give your children an example of how to maximize their potential for the Lord and it will give you opportunity to discipleship your children in a "real world" setting not likely available to you as an employee working for "the Man."

Having your own business on the side should also make it easier for you to stand on your own two feet financially. This is important because a man of Christ should model financial responsibility to his family. Certainly, there are times when money is tight and a little help from family or friends is appreciated; I'm not saying you should stiff arm any offer of financial help from outside your household. However, that should not be the norm. You need to be financially independent and if "ministry work" is cutting into the time you need to earn a living, you need to cut back on the ministry.

A man of Christ must also be hospitable and

*Kingdom Practicalities*

look for opportunities to serve others. Include your family in these endeavors and use those service opportunities to discover the gifts your wife and children have. That is one of your primary responsibilities: find out what God has put into each member of your family and help them cultivate and maximize those things for the sake of the kingdom. God has given you the wife and children you have for a reason. Their particular gifts - indeed, simply the people they are - are designed to fortify your own call and ensure the continuity of the kingdom of God. Your wife is oriented to you as you are oriented to your task. Your children will learn how to pursue the particular work God has for them as they work alongside you in bringing your arena of responsibility under the authority of Jesus Christ.

### Church Practicalities

Before a man of Christ can serve in his local church he must get his own house in order. I proceed on the assumption you understand that.

The first step in serving at your church is to find the job no one else wants to do. At this point you don't need to worry about your particular gifts; you just need to be willing to get your hands dirty. At the same time, if you're not confident with your handyman skills, you might want to leave the rewiring of the sanctuary to someone else and volunteer to be the "go-for" instead. In other words, make a conscious effort to be helpful in the last place rather than the first.

After you have some time under your belt doing grunt work around the church you can begin to look for ways to use your particular gifts in service to Christ's body. This doesn't necessarily mean you'll join the church board and become the treasurer or something like that. I'm talking about looking for unmet needs in the local fellowship that *you* can meet. These might be needs no one has even considered. For instance, it may be that no one has thought about starting a Boy Scout troop, with the church as sponsor and godly men from your fellowship as leaders. It might be no one has thought about offering reading instruction to the community (using the Bible and other Christian works as textbooks). Perhaps no one has considered it necessary to assemble a group of men and boys who will provide free yard care to neighborhood senior citizens and shut-ins who are not a part of the church. I think you get the idea. There are plenty of things your local church could be doing if there were willing workers ready to shoulder the task.

All of this must be done under the authority of church leadership. So, take the time to create a detailed plan, supporting your idea with properly applied Scripture and make it clear that you will take all responsibility for getting the job done. Then take the idea to the elders and get their approval. Submit to the decision of church leadership even if the determination is not what you hoped for. One of the tasks of church leadership is to define the specific mission of the local Body and if your idea does not fit with that mission, then they have the responsibility to put on the brakes and you have the responsibility to submit. However, unless you have some cockeyed idea you are trying to pass off as "community ministry," the chances are your church leadership will be thrilled to give you the go-ahead.

You should also take part in the men's fellowship at your church. If you do not have a men's fellowship at your church, prayerfully consider start-

*Kingdom Practicalities*

ing one. I'm not talking about a weekly meeting where everybody gets together to spill their guts in a Promise Keepers style group therapy session. I'm talking about a once monthly gathering of church men to hear teaching from the elders and have a respectful question-and-answer time concerning doctrine, the particular mission of the church, opportunities for ministry and so on. Start this kind of thing by approaching the church leaders with your idea and volunteering to be the one who takes care of all the logistics.

As I conclude this section I want to touch on the topic of serving as an elder or deacon in your local church. In the first place, you should not consider yourself a viable candidate for either task unless you can honestly meet the criteria presented in 1 Timothy 3:1-13 and Titus 1:5-9. This is so even if others in the church approach you with a request that you stand for election (assuming that is how your church does things). The man of Christ will not seek after something he is not qualified to do.

If you meet the requirements given in Scripture and end up serving as an elder or deacon, you will then have the responsibility to do all these things we have talked about so far - even better! Truly, every Christian man should strive to meet the qualifications for leadership outlined in 1 Timothy and Titus. Whether you serve as an elder or deacon or not, you will do well to be the man of Christ that Paul describes in these two letters.

### Community Practicalities

No matter where in life a man of Christ finds himself, he must exercise servant leadership. Part of that is providing an example that others can imitate. Therefore, in your contact with the community you must always be honest and reliable. You must never back down from truth but you need to express the Gospel in as winsome a fashion as possible.

Your primary contact with the community will probably be as an employee of a business or as a business owner. A working man spends most of his life in the marketplace. Hence, work is where you have the best opportunity to demonstrate how a man lives when he is under the lordship of Jesus. As an employee you need to be the kind of man any employer would love to have working for him. This goes beyond simple honesty and punctuality. Those things are very important but the Christian man must also learn to take hold of creation, tear it apart and rearrange it so it is better than it was when he found it (see, James Jordan, *Through New Eyes: Developing A Biblical View Of The World*). Look at your job, understand it, think of ways to improve your own performance and the overall productivity of the firm and then put it into practice (under the headship of your employer of course). My brother is a good example of this principal. For many years he was employed as a warehouseman in the pharmaceutical business, wrestling pallets and totes every night at the distribution center of a giant of the industry. But that isn't all he did. He also took time to learn the business and think about how he might improve the system. To make a long story short, he eventually started his own company providing services and products of his own invention to pharmaceutical industry. He work-ed hard while he was an employee, carefully considered how that job might be made more efficient and eventually took hold of it, "tore it apart" and reassembled it so it was better than before. A man of Christ does this in

*Kingdom Practicalities*

imitation of his heavenly Father. This is what God did when he made the universe. He brought matter into being out of nothing and then began to "rework it." Each day of creation reveals Yahweh "taking hold" of the stuff he created, rearranging it and making it better. Each day we see our Father declaring his rearrangement of matter "good." This is the model a man of Christ must follow in the workplace.

After you have established godly work habits, look further afield for ways to manifest the kingdom in your community. You can do this by joining existing community organizations and pitching in to serve where there is a need. Be sure to screen the organization so you do not join yourself to something contrary to the kingdom. Your service in these community organizations will be like the service you provide at your church. In other words, be willing to do the grunt work and as your willingness to get the job done becomes known you can expect other opportunities to open.

Do not limit yourself to existing community organizations. You might want to start something new like a Christian businessman's group with a focus on community service.

You should also get involved in local government. You might attend city Council meetings and speak out from a kingdom perspective on the issues that concern your community. Or, you may find God calls you to run for local office. In either case you must know what the Bible says about civil government. As we have seen, civil magistrates are servants of God and must obey him in their work as civic leaders. If you want to get involved in politics in any way, you will be required to study the Word to understand how to apply biblical principles of civil governance in the 21$^{st}$ century. If you believe God is calling you to serve him in politics, you need to start by reading the books listed in the addendum. Very few people in the church today understand what the Bible has to say about civil government. Most Christians don't believe the Bible has much of anything to say about civil government in the twenty-first century. A minority believes the Old Testament law should be applied to modern society without alteration. A still smaller minority understands that all of God's principals are valid all the time and they need to be applied to modern society in light of the basic truth that we live in the age of the Son of Man. This is the bottom line: before you run for political office, get an education in kingdom political theory.

You probably recognize there is a desperate need to bring the rule of Jesus Christ to bear in your community. Perhaps you understand there is no such thing as neutrality and that every society rests upon a religious foundation of one sort or another. Until Christians accept the fact that there is only one workable foundation for any society and the foundation that works is the kingdom of God, Christianity will remain of little consequence outside the Christian ghetto. I am not talking about ushering in the kingdom by force. It doesn't happen that way. The kingdom of God is realized as individuals come under the authority of Jesus Christ and then labor to bring their sphere of influence under his authority. This *must* happen no matter what your arena of activity might be.

If you are a doctor, bring your sphere of influence under Christ's authority and work out your salvation in fear and trembling in the field of medical science. If you are a carpenter, submit your sphere of influence to the Lord Jesus Christ and work heartily as unto the Lord. If you are an elected official, govern in submission to the king of the universe. Know what is good governance and what is bad governance - what is good law and what is bad law - according to God's Word. There is no alternative for the man of Christ. Self-government under God must eventually lead to national government under God.

### *Kingdom Practicalities, Conclusion*

This chapter is not supposed to be a comprehensive treatment of the subject of practical kingdom living. Nor does one size fits all in the kingdom of God. For instance, one man may be called to run a business, lead a community service group and stand for public office. Another man of Christ might be called to be a top notch employee and write thoughtful letters to the editor on occasion. Each is responsible for what God has given him. Meanwhile, understand that every man of Christ must at least meet the basic requirements outlined in the sections on individual and family practicalities. Beyond that, your specific work for the Lord depends on who God has made you, where he has placed you and who he has working along side you. Ultimately your work in the kingdom depends upon how Christ decides to use you. In any case, whatever you do, do all to the glory of God - and don't be discouraged if it takes longer than you expect.

# CHAPTER 7
## THE OPPORTUNITY OF OUR TIME

*They shall not hurt nor destroy in all My holy mountain, For the earth shall be full of the knowledge of the LORD As the waters cover the sea* (Isaiah 11:9)

The Bible tells us the people of God can expect to be blessed when they live in obedience to God's Word. Yet there are those who suggest the promises of Deuteronomy chapter 28 (for instance) do not apply to the church but are reserved for ethnic Israel. However, a careful reading of Scripture makes it clear that the covenant relationship we enjoy today is the same as has existed from the beginning of time. When Peter stood up the day of Pentecost and preached the gospel of salvation in Jesus Christ he was not inventing a new religion but was calling his countrymen to participate in the realization of the covenant promises made to the patriarchs.

Likewise the apostle Paul says, *You are all sons of God through faith in Christ Jesus; for all of you who have been baptized into Christ, have clothed yourselves with Christ. In Him the distinc-*

*tions between Jew and Gentile, slave and free man, male and female, disappear; you are all one in Christ Jesus. And if you belong to Christ, then you are indeed true descendants of Abraham, and are heirs in fulfillment of the promise* (Galatians 3:29, Weymouth Translation). This means God does not discriminate according to ethnic origin or national identity. Instead, all of God's promises are yes to all those who are in Christ Jesus (2 Corinthians 1:20).

There are those who suggest we must take our cue on how to proceed from the current state of affairs. We are told to simply look around and face the reality of a failing church. Most of these pessimists have been taught from an early age that the best they can hope for is an any-moment rapture. After all, it is far easier (in one sense) if defeat and failure for the church have been ordained.

On the other hand, the Bible teaches a theology of optimism. In fact, there are only two views one may have concerning the gospel. One view says the gospel will fail and the other says the gospel of salvation in Jesus Christ will succeed. One view says no matter how far and wide the gospel of Christ is preached it will not have the effect on this world it was designed to have. The other point of view says we should be preaching the gospel to everyone we can because the good news of salvation in Jesus Christ will win converts, will discipline the nations and will one day cover the earth as the waters cover the sea (Isaiah 11:9).

It would have been easier if God had not chosen to work through human agents. If God so desired, he could simply determine that at a certain point in history all of mankind would bend the knee in unfeigned submission to the Creator of the universe. If God wanted, he could "snap his fingers" and change the hearts of every man, woman and child on the face of the earth. However, that is not what God decided to do. Instead, God chose to extend his reign through the activities of his human representatives. It is through our obedience to the faith that the kingdom of God is realized in this realm.

Furthermore, it is wrong for us to believe Satan is the ruler of this world. Not long before his ascension, Jesus told his disciples, *All power in Heaven and over the earth has been given to me. Go therefore and make disciples of all the nations; baptize them into the name of the Father, and of the Son, and of the Holy Spirit; and teach them to obey every command which I have given you. And remember, I am with you always, day by day, until the Close of the Age* (Matthew 28:18-20). Obviously Jesus is claiming authority over *everything*. This doesn't leave room for a kingdom of Satan on this earth. I am not suggesting Satan has absolutely no power in this realm but we should realize the devil is chained, restricted from making the kind of mischief he was allowed during the old covenant administration. We live in the age of the Son of Man not in the age of angels. Satan (the fallen angel) has been cast out of heaven where he previously was allowed to accuse the brethren. Instead of an accuser we have an advocate who stands before the throne of God. Satan does not rule in this world – not now or ever again in the future. Jesus Christ's kingdom has been established and it is a kingdom without end. It will take many generations for the kingdom to be fully realized and there may be times when it seems the tide is moving backward but we can rest assured that Christ is the victorious ruler now and forever.

If we hope to participate in Christ's kingdom we need a clear understanding of what he calls us to do. Study the Bible and do so with Christ in mind. Ask the Holy Spirit for illumination. Be true men and get to work.

### The Character Of The Kingdom

Isaiah 11:9 (cited above) is part of a larger passage describing the character of the kingdom of God. We might wonder what Isaiah means when he speaks of this "holy mountain." If we know the words of the prophet we will recognize his reference to an earlier word about the character of the messianic kingdom. Isaiah tells us, *it shall come to pass in the latter days That the mountain of the LORD's house Shall be established on the top of the mountains, And shall be exalted above the hills; And all nations shall flow to it. Many people shall come and say, "Come, and let us go up to the mountain of the LORD, To the house of the God of Jacob; He will teach us His ways, And we shall walk in His paths." For out of Zion shall go forth the law, And the word of the LORD from Jerusalem. He shall judge between the nations, And rebuke many people; They shall beat their swords into plowshares, And their spears into pruning hooks; Nation shall not lift up sword against nation, Neither shall they learn war anymore* (Isaiah 2:2-4).

Thus, the holy mountain represents Christ's rule. It is more than the church or a single location on a map. Instead, the holy mountain is the entire earth. This truth is not realized immediately but as we see in Daniel's prophecy the stone cut without hands (Jesus and his kingdom) will crush all opposing authority and grow to fill the entire earth.

*Men Of Issachar*

This holy mountain of God's kingdom may appear to be restricted to a certain location at certain times in history; or, more accurately, it may be in evidence in a variety of places throughout history. But the eventual outcome will be an overlapping of these different expressions of Christ's rule so there will be a "mountain" covering the whole earth.

To say no one will hurt or destroy in all God's holy mountain does not suggest that the moment a person becomes a believer every old habit falls to the wayside and life is a breeze. It takes time for the leaven of the kingdom to work through the life of the individual just as it takes time for the leaven of Christ's rule to work through society. Indeed, it will take many generations for the fullness of Christ's reign to be accomplished in this life and realm. We will not achieve perfection in this current age. We will move ever closer to a union of heaven and earth but until the final events of history take place, that union will not be complete.

I am not suggesting a return to Eden. Rather, our expectation should exceed the circumstance of the Edenic relationship. This is so because we are in relationship with the father through Jesus Christ. This is a far better situation than that of Adam. Do not fall into the trap of thinking Christ came to patch things up and do his best to reverse the problems introduced by Adam's sin. Certainly Christ came as the last Adam in order to undo the damage done by the first but God had always determined to relate to mankind through his Eternal Son.

In addition, the holy Mountain is established one heart at a time. God's kingdom will *not* be enforced from the top down but is realized as individual hearts are remade. The kingdom of God rests upon a grass roots change in society. It is *never* established by law, coercion or force but only through the willing submission of the saved.

This new state of affairs began with the resurrection of Jesus Christ. Through his resurrection, the new creation burst into the old and began to overcome the curse. In the new life of Jesus Christ, new life of all of mankind was made available. As an individual comes to a saving knowledge of Jesus Christ and is over-whelmed by the Holy Spirit, other people come into contact with the new creation wrought by Jesus when they come into contact with the Believer. As these Believers bring their life under the authority of Christ their families likewise take on the character of the new humanity. Eventually, families that have been brought into a saving relationship with Jesus, will take dominion in their arena of activity and fulfill the cultural mandate given to mankind at the beginning of time.

Therefore the lion, wolf and bear mentioned by the prophet Isaiah just prior to our verse from Isaiah 11:9, do not represent literal beasts who have returned to an Edenic posture. Instead the prophet tells us the kingdom of God changes the heart and character of a man. This can only be true if we understand the gospel of Jesus Christ as something more than mere fire insurance. It is not designed just to save us from eternal torment; it is primarily designed to make us instruments of God's use for reconciling creation back to the Creator. This is accomplished as lion, wolf and bear like men submit themselves to the objective standards of God's Word. These beast-like men become servants of the most high God and their character is shaped to his use.

The newly made men described in this passage are expected to regulate their behavior in terms of God's written word. This is impossible without the illumination and empowering presence of the Holy Spirit and also impossible apart from an understanding of God's law. We are called to imitate our heavenly father and our "older brother" Jesus Christ. In doing so we will live a life of obedience to God's Word. This obedience will be measured against the word by the church which holds the plumb-line of Scripture against the lives of God's people. This is not a condemning ministry but a nurturing ministry of discipline and correction. Later, when the holy mountain is more evident, we can expect to see nations make use of Scripture in creating God honoring civil governments. Again, this does not mean the state is given the responsibility to make Christian converts or to govern the conscience in any way. Instead, we simply acknowledge the fact that the state is a minister of God and as such must make use of his Word in legislation and keeping the peace.

Additionally, we cannot fall into the trap of thinking this is merely a matter of destiny or fate. As I mentioned earlier God's people are blessed for their obedience. On the other hand, they can expect to be punished for disobedience: *And you have forgotten the exhortation which speaks to you as to sons: "MY SON, DO NOT DESPISE THE CHASTENING OF THE LORD, NOR BE DISCOURAGED WHEN YOU ARE REBUKED BY HIM; FOR WHOM THE LORD LOVES HE CHASTENS, AND SCOURGES EVERY SON WHOM HE RECEIVES." If you endure chastening, God deals with you as with sons; for what son is there whom a Father does not chasten? But if you are without chastening, of which all have become partakers, then you are illegitimate and not*

*The Opportunity Of Our Times*

*sons* (Hebrews 12:5-8). Through this process of discipline, God's people come to an understanding of how they are supposed to walk out their salvation. This process teaches people of God the meaning of victory and serves to turn their eyes of God's to the Heavenly father. It is also a logical consequence of God's choice to work through human agents.

One might object, saying this sounds like works salvation. It may appear that I am suggesting we can work our way to utopia. But that is exactly the opposite of what I have in mind. The Bible teaches, *by grace you have been saved through faith, and that not of yourselves; it is the gift of God, not of works, lest anyone should boast. For we are His workmanship, created in Christ Jesus for good works, which God prepared before-hand that we should walk in them* (Ephesians 2:8-10). There is no place for works salvation in the economy of God. It is unbiblical and, indeed, impossible. Instead, we are saved by grace so we might serve our heavenly Father with good works.

The Bible teaches that salvation and works are related. The Bible also makes it very clear that our salvation is a gift from God. Our new birth is not dependent upon any works we may do. Nevertheless, works and salvation are bound together. Take note of verse ten in the passage cited above; we are the workmanship of God, created in Christ *for good works*. In other words, we are not our own workmanship - we do not have anything to do with procuring our own salvation - but we are the work of God in Christ. And he created us in Christ for a purpose; to do good works. Indeed, God prepared beforehand (predestined before our creation in Christ) the good works we should do. The point is

*Men Of Issachar*

that when God creates someone anew in Christ (2 Corinthians 5:17), the result is a follower of Jesus who produces good works. After all, faith without works is dead (James 2:20). One might say good works are one part of the whole of predestination. This doesn't mean we will live a perfect life after our new birth. God doesn't choreograph our lives so that every waking moment is some sort of a "good work." It *does* mean good works - be they many or few – are part of the pack-age.

No individual member of the kingdom is a cookie cutter copy of another. God draws one man through a life of trial and tribulation while another may live a life of comparative ease. One man may seem to be a veritable fountain of good works while the next may produce hardly a trickle of charitable deeds in his life. Yet as Paul says in another place; "who are you to judge another man's servant?" It is the *presence* of good works that concern both James and Paul. The quantity or quality of good works is not a matter for us to judge.

Paul states that salvation is a gracious gift embraced by faith and includes foreordained good works. James picks up on this idea and comes to the logical conclusion that saving faith is accompanied by good works - faith without works is dead. Neither is saying nor means to say salvation is earned through works. But both would say election *and* good works are predestined.

The arena where God's absolute sovereignty is easiest to understand and accept is in the process of salvation. Everything depends upon God because the natural human heart hates God and is at war with Him (Romans 8:7 etc.). No one can do anything to save himself. Smith's heart is corrupt and unable to

*The Opportunity Of Our Times*

submit to God. He does not *want* to submit to God and *will not* submit to God in his natural sinful condition. Even if Smith does recognize the existence of sin he does not believe he needs to repent of his sin before God. Smith is free to act in anyway his will may dictate but it is impossible for him to act in a manner contradictory to his basic nature. Since Smith cannot act in a manner that contradicts his sinful nature he is powerless to do anything to effect his own salvation. However, once the Holy Spirit has given him a new heart, Smith is both willing and able to repent of his sin and submit to Christ. The Bible teaches these truths clearly and so there should be no difficulty understanding the total sovereignty of God in producing a new creation.

The problem is that we humans are unable to understand how a man can apparently exercise free will and still be under the sovereign control of God. No one *really* understands how that can be; nor do we really understand how God can be three *and* one. Nevertheless these things are true. So, every man, whether born again or lost, acts according to his nature and does so as his own will dictates. At the same time, God is the one who controls the outcome. *A man's heart plans his way but the Lord directs his steps* (Proverbs 16:9. See also Proverbs 16:33, 21:1, 31). In short, God uses Smith in a way that accords to Smith's nature (good or bad), in accomplishing His will even while Smith exercises *his* free will.

Thus even though God foreordains the good works of his people, those good works take place as the true follower of Christ determines *in his own heart* to do what his Lord requires of him. His good works are not coerced, but arise naturally out of the love and gratitude he feels for Jesus his Lord and

Savior. Even still, he won't always do what is right. As Paul tells us, the very thing we want to do as new creations in Christ we often do not do. This is why Paul tells the church at Philippi to, *work out your own salvation with fear and trembling; for it is God who works in you both to will and to do for His good pleasure* (Philippians 2:12-13).

So, put forth every effort to produce the fruit of the new creation even as you acknowledge it is *God* who gives you the desire and the ability to do what he requires. He does this in the first place by making us a new creation able to do good. He does this in the second place by actively empowering us on a daily basis with the presence of his Holy Spirit. In any case, true, saving faith will result in good works.

Although salvation is a gift it does require "assembly" to be fully appreciated. This is why we are called upon to cultivate the new creation in order to express what God has done for us. We know we are assembling the gift of salvation properly when we follow the instructions found in the Bible. God's law guides us in the cultivation of the new creation and the expression of good works tell the world we are members of the body of Jesus Christ.

Thus the holy mountain of Isaiah 11:9 is characterized by humans who have become a new creation in Jesus Christ and express that relationship through obedience to their God and Savior, which results in an exercise of dominion in their arena of activity. They bring their sphere of influence under the authority of Jesus Christ as they do *everything* as unto the Lord.

## The Reach Of The Kingdom

I am not talking about universal salvation. The Scripture plainly teaches that many will refuse to

## The Opportunity Of Our Times

accept Jesus Christ as Lord and Savior. Ezekiel gives us a picture of this truth when he tells us about the river flowing from the Temple, bringing life wherever it goes (Ezekiel 47:1-12). However, not all waters are healed by this stream. Some areas are left as salt marshes. In other words, even though the mountain of the Lord will cover the whole earth there will be those who refuse the offer of salvation. This tells us Ezekiel's vision concerns this age and is a prophecy of both optimism and doom: optimism concerning the victory of the Gospel and doom for those who refuse to repent.

Yet Isaiah says that *the earth shall be full of the knowledge of the Lord as the waters cover the sea.* This implies all of mankind will be touched by the reign of the Messiah. This much is true. Although we do not believe in universal salvation we do accept the fact that all of mankind will be influenced by the reign of Christ. Think of it this way: everyone swimming in a pool is affected by the presence of water in that swimming area. Now, if there are 100 people in the pool and 90 of them are bailing water out while 10 are replenishing the pool from an outside source we should expect the water level to gradually drop. On the other hand, if 90 people in the pool are replenishing the water and only 10 are trying to bail it out, we should expect the water level to remain stable or indeed rise. This illustrates how the knowledge of the Lord can cover the earth as the waters cover the sea even though some people reject Christ. In a predominantly Christian society, where most of the people are born again and working to bring their sphere of influence under the control of Jesus, the blessings of a life under the authority of Christ will be realized (to a certain extent) by

*Men Of Issachar*

everyone in that society. Even though some of the people are trying to "bail out" the influence of the kingdom they will enjoy its benefits. I realize this illustration is not without faults but it does help us to understand how the kingdom can have a broad reach even when there are people - perhaps many people - who do not receive Christ as Savior.

The filling of the pool, this expansion of the kingdom, takes place as individuals and their families come to a saving knowledge of Jesus Christ and live under the authority of the King. Remember, Paul tells us the blessings of kingdom citizenship are extended even to non-believing members of the household. Certainly this is a benefit, but our hope is that all members of a household touched by the Gospel would come to know Jesus Christ personally. When this happens that household will begin to exercise dominion in its sphere of influence and increase the godly impact through their personal lives and that of the family unit. This process will be multiplied as churches teach individuals and families their responsibility in the kingdom economy. This process will further expand as new churches are planted and the lost are evangelized and made to understand the comprehensive nature of the Gospel. As this continues we should see the influence of the ungodly rolled back. This will not happen by armed revolution but through the changed lives of individuals and families. One of the things we should see is a wholesale abandonment of the public school system by Christians. We have talked about this so I will simply say that a Christian should never subject his children to godless education system.

When I was much younger I believed I would live to see the kingdom of God realized in its fullness.

## The Opportunity Of Our Times

I believed the grassroots revolution would happen very quickly and that my children would have the privilege of growing up in a world where the knowledge of the Lord covered the earth as the waters cover the sea. I have subsequently come to the understanding that this process of dominion will take many generations. Men of Christ today must understand their job is to build a solid foundation for the generations to come. Or perhaps it would be more accurate to say our job is to reinforce the foundation we have inherited from our forefathers. We cannot expect God's kingdom to be realized according to our time table. We must submit to the timing of our Father in heaven.

It may seem like there is no progress being made. To our human eyes it may seem that the Kingdom is *not* advancing in this age. An antidote to this pessimism is a good knowledge of Bible history. One need only read the Gospel accounts describing the state the disciples were in after Christ was crucified. A disinterested observer would not have given the infant church much chance for survival. Nonetheless, those few, frightened people in the upper room on the day of Pentecost were the foundation stones for a church numbering in the billions today. Our problem is spiritual nearsightedness. We view history through the eyes of man rather than the eyes of God. Rather than look to the wisdom of the world we need to know our Bible and understand *God's* plan for victory.

In light of this we must reject the idea that the failure of the Gospel and the advent of the Antichrist is in our future. In the first place, this contradicts the plain teaching of Scripture concerning the victory of Christ's kingdom. Secondly, the Bible tells us that there is no single antichrist but that *any* person who leaves the faith is an antichrist. According to John, many antichrists were evident in the last days of the old covenant age: *Little children, it is the last hour; and as you have heard that the antichrist is coming, even now many antichrists have come, by which we know that it is the last hour. They went out from us, but they were not of us; for if they had been of us, they would have continued with us; but they went out that they might be made manifest, that none of them were of us* (1 John 2:18-19). Thus, we should not worry about a coming Antichrist or Beast who will set up a one world government. There never will be a one world human government. Moreover, the Beast of Scripture is no longer active. The Beast spirit animated the kingdoms responsible for disciplining the people of God. According to The Revelation, that spirit was cast into the lake of fire with the manifestation of Christ's kingdom in the first century (Revelation 19:20).

Even in the fullness of the messianic kingdom there will not be a one world government. In other words, there will never be a single governing bureaucracy holding sway over the entire earth. Instead, in the kingdom of God, nations will retain their separate identity as they individually submit to Jesus, the universal king (Isaiah 2:2-4).

In addition, there will not be a single *form* of government required in the kingdom of the Messiah. Nowhere do we find a command saying "thou shalt have a democracy" or "thou shalt establish a representative form of government" and so on. Instead, the kingdom of God will be characterized by separate nations, governing themselves according to their choice under the authority of the King of the universe.

Our responsibility as men of Christ is to live a life of obedience to God's word. We must be faithful to what we see in the Scripture. The Bible says, *as you therefore have received Christ Jesus the Lord, so walk in him, rooted and built up in him and established in the faith, as you have been taught, abounding in it with thanksgiving* (Colossians 2:6-7). We received the Lord Jesus Christ by faith and so we must live our life in faith. We receive the Lord Jesus Christ as our master and so must live a life acknowledging his lordship. This can be accomplished only if we are rooted in him and built up in him. This happens as we dig into the Word and cry out to God to be energized and illuminated by the Holy Spirit. This takes place as we strive to imitate our Savior, bringing glory to him in every aspect of our life. Finally, we know the kingdom of God will cover the earth as the waters cover the sea in this age because the Bible tells us so.

### *According To God's Will*

The section of Isaiah's prophecy we have been discussing is prefaced by the declaration, *Therefore thus says the Lord God of hosts* (Isaiah 10:24). It tells us that God has ordained victory for the Messianic kingdom. Remember, the Bible promises blessings for those who live a life of obedience to God: *Now it shall come to pass, if you diligently obey the voice of the LORD your God, to observe carefully all His commandments which I command you today, that the LORD your God will set you high above all nations of the earth. And all these blessings shall come upon you and overtake you, because you obey the voice of the LORD your God* (Deuteronomy 28:1-2). These promises are given to the people of God in every age. There is no Jew nor Greek in the kingdom of God. In Christ, all are heirs of the promise. In Christ we have been grafted into the root and stock of Israel (Romans 11:17) and so the promises extended to Israel are ours as well (see, D. Eric Williams, *The End Was Near*). This is not to say Israel has been replaced but that Israel has been greatly expanded in Jesus the Christ. Indeed, the true Israel is Christ our Lord. This is why Paul can say without equivocation that everyone who is in Jesus Christ will participate in the promises given to the patriarchs.

Without this point of view it is impossible to remain faithful to the Word of God. If we suggest God has had a variety of plans over the ages, we deny the unchanging quality of his character. The Bible tells us Jesus is the same today, yesterday and forever (Hebrews 13:8). Therefore we understand that God's plan for creation has never changed. Certainly the covenant has enjoyed a variety of administrations but it has remained one covenant from the beginning of time until now.

Contrary to what some "Bible teachers" may suggest this point of view is in no way anti-Semitic. The biblical point of view excludes no one from the offer of salvation. The biblical point of view recognizes God's chosen people are defined as those redeemed by Jesus Christ. The first century church was largely Jewish and Jews have been part of the body of Christ ever since. To suggest God has two chosen people with two different covenants is to make God of two minds. We reject this dualistic approach to God's covenant relationship and recognize that the Gentile nations have been grafted into Israel in Jesus Christ.

I realize it may cost you fellowship to embrace

*The Opportunity Of Our Times*

this view of the kingdom. You will find yourself bludgeoned with the opinions of "the experts" and so I warn you to have your ducks in a row before you share this point of view with others. Resolve to stand for the truth and do so with love and humility. I'm not suggesting you should leave a particular church over this issue; that will be between you and the Lord. In fact, I would counsel you to stay put and work out your salvation where God has placed you.

It boils down to our responsibility to obey God rather than men. You may have been raised in a church that preaches defeat and ignores God's law. You may feel the cost is too high and radical changes in theology such as this are better left to other men. If you feel this way I urge you to reconsider. The crisis of our time is an opportunity for the people of God. Yet, we will squander this opportunity if we do not submit ourselves to the King of Kings. Men of Christ must rise up and take hold of their God-given responsibility. To do otherwise is to fear man rather than God.

### *Conclusion*

Throughout this book I have emphasized the need for Christian men to take responsibility for their own lives. There is no excuse for Christian men who fail to overcome sin in their life. We are not of two natures, as if battling the old man in an effort to live a life in imitation of Jesus Christ. Rather, we are a new creation in Christ. There is an impression left behind by the old man but that impression may be overcome in the power of the Holy Spirit as we submit our lives to our Lord. It is our duty to clear out the trash left behind by the old nature rather than allow it to remain in the "house" where we will periodically trip over it or find ourselves rummaging

*Men Of Issachar*

through it. Every man of Christ must begin with a decision to submit himself fully to the Lord. He must commit himself to living in imitation of Jesus in order to be a man worthy of imitation as well.

Once a man has brought his life into line with the expectations of the Messiah, indeed even while he is doing so, he must strive to bring his family under the authority of Jesus Christ as well. The family is the building block of society and until Christian men do their duty as leaders in their own households, we will not see significant change in this world.

Additionally, men of Christ must step up to the plate of leadership in the local body. We cannot allow the usurpation of male leadership in the church to continue. We cannot allow effeminate men to impress their character upon the body of Christ. We cannot allow our warrior king to be represented by thumb-sucking wimps.

There are many resources men of Christ can draw upon in their efforts to grow in Christlikeness. Make use of the preliminary reading list found in the addendum. From there, you may follow the thread of sources cited in the books in the list.

Men of Christ need to work with others in the task and so I encourage you to approach your pastor and ask him for help in assuming your role as leader in your family, church and community. I am not suggesting you should try to bend your pastor to your will. Instead I suggest you give him a copy of this book or simply ask him to provide you with additional teaching resources as you strive to become a true man of Christ. Also you might offer to put together a men's group for your pastor to lead; offer to do the legwork if he will provide the teaching. If

*The Opportunity Of Our Times*

your pastor does not have the time for additional study and teaching seek out a mature man in the church and ask him if he would be willing to lead a study group. Do this only with the blessing of your pastor.

Only as a last resort would you leave your church and seek a place where the people of God are working to establish the kingdom. I say this because we are supposed to seek unity in the body. I also believe it is important for men of Christ to be salt and light were the Lord has placed them. Let it never be said that I encouraged men to take their families out of one church and attend another. Instead, I encourage Christian men to labor where they are and do all they can to build up the ministry of the Body they currently attend.

One word will sum up this entire book: obedience. The Bible tells us we must be obedient to the Faith. Indeed, salvation is all about obedience; we must be obedient to the Spirit in order to repent and receive Christ's offer of salvation. Obedience is required as we assemble this gift of salvation and fulfill our responsibility as men of Christ.

# EPILOGUE
## KINGDOM STATUS

*I assure you: Whoever does not welcome the kingdom of God like a little child will never enter it.*
(Luke 18:17, Holman Christian Standard Bible)

Christ's discourse in Matthew 18:1-14 concerning status in the kingdom requires careful thought. We must study this passage in the context of the whole of Scripture, looking at these words of Jesus in light of what he has said elsewhere. We need to guard against drawing upon this one sermon in isolation to develop doctrine. Any conclusions we arrive at here must be checked against the rest of Scripture.

Now, the connection with the earlier pericope is found in Christ's statement that the sons of the King are free from tax or tribute. This seems to indicate to the other disciples that Peter was considered a son of the king. All the disciples may have thought of themselves in this sense. Yet, Peter's part in the drama concerning the temple tribute seemed to signal he had a special relationship with Jesus. And the "temple tax incident" would have reinforced other events pointing to Peter's preeminence among

## Kingdom Status

the apostles. Yet, Matthew 18:1-14 reminds us the kingdom of God is not about status. It is not about who is in charge. We are reminded there is a certain attitude one must have in order to be part of the kingdom of God. We are reminded that little children seem to understand their place in the grand scheme of things. In other words, Jesus does not use a child as an example because children are naturally good; he uses the child as an example because little children are naturally without status or authority - and little children (especially those raised in a godly home) generally accept their station in life.

Furthermore it is important to keep the historical context in mind. Jesus is speaking to his apostles in the context of the first century Jewish mission. If we remember that, we will be better able to make application to all believers in this New Testament age.

So, in Matthew 18 we read, *At that time the disciples came to Jesus, saying, "Who then is greatest in the kingdom of heaven?" Then Jesus called a little child to Him, set him in the midst of them, and said, "Assuredly, I say to you, unless you are converted and become as little children, you will by no means enter the kingdom of heaven. Therefore whoever humbles himself as this little child is the greatest in the kingdom of heaven. Whoever receives one little child like this in My name receives Me. Whoever causes one of these little ones who believe in Me to sin, it would be better for him if a millstone were hung around his neck, and he were drowned in the depth of the sea. Woe to the world because of offenses! For offenses must come, but woe to that man by whom the offense comes! If your hand or foot causes you to sin, cut it off and cast it from you. It is better for you to enter into life lame or maimed, rather than having two hands or two feet, to be cast into the everlasting fire. And if your eye causes you to sin, pluck it out and cast it from you. It is better for you to enter into life with one eye, rather than having two eyes, to be cast into hell fire. Take heed that you do not despise one of these little ones, for I say to you that in heaven their angels always see the face of My Father who is in heaven. For the Son of Man has come to save that which was lost. What do you think? If a man has a hundred sheep, and one of them goes astray, does he not leave the ninety-nine and go to the mountains to seek the one that is straying? And if he should find it, assuredly, I say to you, he rejoices more over that sheep than over the ninety-nine that did not go astray. Even so it is not the will of your Father who is in heaven that one of these little ones should perish"* (Matthew 18:1-14).

This portion of Scripture tells us that little ones who are scandalized must be retrieved.

### Little Ones

According to Mark's account, the apostles were disputing among themselves about who was the greatest as they walked toward Capernaum. They thought they had hidden this discussion from Jesus so they were reluctant to say anything to him about it upon arriving at the house. Matthew says the disciples eventually asked Jesus *who then is the greatest in the kingdom of heaven?* I find it incredible this was on the minds of the apostles at this point in time. Jesus had talked to them about his death and resurrection a number of times by now and it would seem *that* topic would be of more interest to the apostles than their status in the

## Kingdom Status

kingdom. I think status came up in the discussion because of the things that had gone on just prior to this. It appeared to anyone who might care to look, that Peter was in line to be the head honcho after Jesus was gone. Perhaps talk about Jesus death and resurrection *did* play a part in this because if Christ were going to die, then someone else would be left in charge. Peter seemed to be the most likely choice. In any case, the other apostles probably didn't like the prospect so an argument began concerning greatness in the kingdom. Once again we are reminded that the apostles were very immature at this point. Clearly, Jesus did not choose them to be his closest followers because of their superior understanding and maturity. He chose them because they had character qualities he could shape as he wanted. The maturity would come later.

Once the truth about the roadway discussion was discovered, Jesus called a little child and set him in the midst of the apostles. Mark tells us the little child was called in and set in the midst of them - perhaps for a moment - and then Jesus took the child into his arms before he taught them concerning rank in the Messianic kingdom (Mark 9:33-37). Children in first century Jewish culture were highly valued - there is no question about that. In fact, it was considered a curse to be childless. At the same time, children were expected to be seen and not heard. So, it was not a matter of value but status that Jesus wanted to emphasize when he called a child into the meeting. I can imagine the introduction of this little child into the group (the Greek is *paidion* which means little child or even infant) would have caused an offense and ruffled the feathers of most of the apostles. I have seen this kind of thing before. When

*Men Of Issachar*

big things are going on, who wants little kids or other unimportant folk hanging around? So, I imagine some of the apostles took umbrage at this breach of decorum. After all, Jesus was showing honor to a child who had no status in society in the sense that he had no influence or authority at all.

Then Jesus shocked his apostles. He told them that unless they were converted and became as little children *they* would not enter the kingdom of heaven. Frankly this *is* a rather shocking statement. He says they must have the same view of status a little child or an infant might have in order to be part of the messianic kingdom. This is not about the morality or behavior of a child. Anyone who has children knows little children are not without sin. It is not as if a baby is born a blank slate and is innocent until taught to do wrong. Indeed, every human being is born in a state of depravity and naturally commits personal sin as well.

The point is that the apostles must have *no* concern for status in the grand scheme of things just as a little child is not concerned with the fact his parents are in charge. Indeed, a child is pleased his parents are in charge. He will often take advantage of that (which can sometimes be a sinful thing to do) but he does not chafe at the bit and hope for greater status in the family. That kind of attitude usually comes later. But a little child is more than happy to be the "littlest" and the one with no status or authority. This does not come naturally to an adult. Human beings are naturally self-centered and it is typical for adults to strive for status in their circle of influence. Most adults want to be seen as something special and be in charge to some extent. In the context of our passage, the apostles were clearly

*Kingdom Status*

concerned with their place in the kingdom. Apparently not many of them would be content with a lesser position; it appears most wanted to be in charge. This is why Jesus says they must turn around - they must undergo a complete change - or they will be left out altogether.

According to Jesus, a person without a childlike lack of concern over status and authority cannot enter the kingdom of God. This is a sensational statement. Jesus says you will not be ruled by him unless you let go of your desire for authority. To ignore this is to rebel against Jesus. As we shall see later, refusal to embrace a childlike view of rank implies a person is not even born again. The true believer will recognize God has determined humility as the proper attitude for a citizen of the kingdom. Indeed, if one is not willing to accept a position of no importance, they are not members of God's household but are part of the family of Satan instead. There is no middle ground. Either a man leaves the Adamic family and enters the family of God in Christ or he does not. To be in the family of God is to be under the authority of Jesus Christ. And Jesus says if you do not become like a little child, you are not under his authority. To be born again includes conversion to a childlike view of status.

It is critical for the apostles to understand the need to humble themselves and be like little children. This sort of Christlike attitude requires violent action from the believer. Of course I do not mean physical violence; I'm talking about the kind of violence Jesus speaks of when he says the kingdom of God suffers violence and violent men take it by force. In other words, the actualization of Christ's rule requires one to rid himself of anything contrary to that rule. This

*Men Of Issachar*

will be humiliating to some (perhaps most) people. To wrap a towel around your waist and wash the feet of your "underlings" would cause unbearable humiliation for most people. And before we say it would be a humiliation simply because of the cultural difference I suggest that *any* such behavior, culturally normal or not, would be humiliating to those who are unwilling to come under the Lord-ship of Jesus Christ and accept a position of no status in the kingdom.

The paradox is that the person who is willing to humble himself as a child will become great in the kingdom. In the Greek it means he will be the elder, the stronger or the greater one among his brethren. This is a paradox because we, along with the apostles, cannot really comprehend how one can be the least while one is great. That is because we think of greatness and status in worldly terms. But in the kingdom of God, to be great is to be servant of all. This is kingdom reality versus worldly reality. It is only when we are in a state of humility that we are useful to God. Only when we have a childlike attitude of indifference concerning status do we truly emulate Jesus Christ.

If we have this attitude we will accept others who share the "status-free" lifestyle. And really, it would be impossible to do so without childlike humility. In Matthew 18:5 Jesus says whoever receives one such little child in my name receives me. Christ used the child in the midst of the apostles as an example but he did not limit his discussion to literal children and infants. The apostles understood this and we need to do the same. This is not about children only. It certainly includes children (who are in Jesus Christ) but it is directed at adults

*Kingdom Status*

who need a childlike attitude about status. Therefore, Jesus says if you (an adult apostle) have this attitude of humility you will receive other members of the Messianic community who have the same attitude of humility. When you do this, Jesus says, you will be receiving me. When you are in fellowship with someone in the family of disciples you are in fellowship with Jesus. However, this must be sincere fellowship. It must be a true love for the brothers and sisters in the company of disciples. It must be unfeigned humility and an eagerness to serve others and associate with others of like mind.

    It is interesting to note that Jesus tells his apostles they receive him when they receive a fellow disciple who is "little" in the kingdom. This is similar to the proclamation found in Matthew chapter 25 concerning the final judgment. There Christ tells the apostles that those who minister to fellow believers who are hungry, thirsty, strangers, naked, sick or in prison are actually ministering to him. This reminds us that the people of Christ are so closely identified with him that what is done to them is actually done to him. We see this truth demonstrated in Jesus' words to Saul when he was confronted by the Lord on the way to Damascus. He asked Saul (later called Paul) why he was persecuting *him*. In other words, persecution of the fledgling church was actually a persecution of Jesus Christ himself.

    I want to emphasize that the total change Jesus demanded of his apostles would not take place without effort. Yet, it is a grace of God; it is impossible for natural man to let go of the desire for status. Even those people who appear to have no interest in social standing, status or authority really do care about those things. They may not seek it for themselves yet they may attach themselves to others who have status or importance in their circle of friends. Or their lack of concern about status may be feigned and be part of their strategy for gaining status - as one who is "umble" like Uriah Heep in Dicken's *David Copperfield* was "umble." So they have the same interest in status as anyone else.

This insistence on service and rejection of status seems to conflict with the requirement to take authority and dominion in this realm. They seem to conflict because we do not understand kingdom reality. Anyone who thinks the kingdom of God will advance by worldly means does not understand the reign of Jesus Christ; things will not get done in the Messianic kingdom by those who are aggressive and power hungry. To feel this way reveals an anti-kingdom mindset.

### Who Are Scandalized

According to Jesus, anyone who causes a little one to be scandalized (or to stumble) will pay a heavy price. The little ones are those who are in Jesus Christ and who exemplify a Christlike attitude. No one will be a perfect example of this "little" orientation but I believe Christ is saying that *any* believer is considered a "little one." At this point the Greek is not *paidion* (small child) but *mikros* (small, little). So Jesus is clearly speaking about believers of any age who exhibit this humble attitude and care nothing for status. Any Believer is on the path to becoming "little" and therefore has some "kingdom status." Some people further down the path of Christlike littleness than others but every Christian is a little one.

Jesus is concerned with guarding those who are like little children in their humble attitude be-

*Kingdom Status*

cause *that very attitude makes them vulnerable*. They are not thinking of protecting themselves or their status. Instead they are genuinely interested in the good of the other person and so interact with others with a certain naivete.

As a result they may be caused to stumble. What this actually says is that they may be scandalized. There are varieties of ways the Greek *scandalon* (noun) and *skandalizo* (verb) are used in the New Testament but because of the context and the rest of what Christ has to say about this particular circumstance we understand Jesus is saying that those who scandalize the little ones are causing them to fall to ruin – to lose their salvation. Jesus uses *skandalizo* in a similar sense when he talks about the different types of soil in Matthew chapter thirteen. There he says someone who receives the word of the kingdom on stony ground will falter under tribulation. It means he stumbles to his eternal ruin (see, D. Eric Williams, *Shine Forth As The Sun*). It means he is lost for eternity. In the case of the different types of soil we are not talking about people who were saved and then lose their salvation. We are talking about people who *appear* to be saved because of their initial response the gospel but their subsequent behavior reveals they were not actually born again. In other words, they are not the "little ones" Jesus has in mind in this text.

This is where we run into some trouble. There is no reason to believe that the little ones of Matthew chapter eighteen are not truly born-again. We know this because Jesus says they believe in him. There is nothing in their behavior that would indicate otherwise (unlike the rocky soil of Matthew chapter thirteen). This is why this passage is often understood to say that if you cause a humble and Christlike believer to merely sin you will pay a heavy price. We *can* apply the principle in that way but that is not what Jesus was saying to his apostles. He has something much more profound in mind.

He tells them that if they or any other follower of Christ causes a little one to be scandalized - not just sin but in the sense that they stumble and fall away from the faith - it would be better if the offender had a millstone hung around his neck and were cast into the sea. The Greek text tells us the millstone Jesus has in mind is the large millstone requiring an animal to turn it. Therefore, the scandal caused by an unfeeling disciple is very serious. Certainly Christ uses some hyperbole at this point. He is not saying we should look for scandalmongers so we can execute them in this gruesome fashion. But Jesus is saying that this is so heinous it *deserves* this kind of punishment. Indeed. A quick drowning is preferred to the eternal punishment that awaits them.

This is not the only place in the New Testament that appears to contradict Christ's own words concerning the security of believers. In his first letter to the church in Corinth the apostle Paul was dealing with the issue of meats sacrificed to idols. He told the more knowledgeable members of the church that their eating of idolatrous sacrifices jeopardized the faith of weaker brothers, saying, *and because of your knowledge shall the weak brother perish, for whom Christ died?* (1 Corinthians 8:11). The Greek word translated as perish is *apollumi*, meaning to destroy, to abolish or bring to complete ruin. Paul uses this term elsewhere to describe those who are lost and destined for hell (1 Corinthian's 1:18, 2 Corinthians

*Kingdom Status*

2:15, 4:3) and there is no reason to think he has another outcome in view here. Therefore, it would seem Paul contradicts Christ just as Jesus seems to contradict himself. Clearly we cannot leave the situation in this condition and so we must search elsewhere for a solution.

Since Paul has contributed to our dilemma we will allow Paul's experience to provide a solution.

In Acts chapter twenty-seven we read of Paul's sea voyage to Rome and the storm he encountered, threatening the lives of all who were on board ship. At one point Paul chides the assembled crowd telling them they *should have listened [to Paul] and not have sailed from Crete and incurred this disaster and loss* (Acts 27:21). He goes on to tell them they should take heart, nonetheless, because an angel from God had assured him he would survive the disaster along with everyone else on board ship. Therefore, we have the sure word of the Lord given to Paul and repeated to his assembled shipmates. Yet there was a point sometime later when some of the sailors were seeking to escape from the vessel and Paul said *unless these men stay in the ship you cannot be saved* (Acts 27:31). So which is it? Was God's promise of salvation from the storm open to question? Or does this passage present a principal enabling us to understand Paul's words in 1 Corinthians eight along with Christ's words in Matthew chapter eighteen? Clearly it is the latter. Charles Hodge has this to say about the issue:

> It was absolutely certain that none of Paul's companions in shipwreck was on that occasion to lose his life, because the salvation of the whole company had been predicted and promised; and yet the apostle said that if the sailors were allowed to take away the boats, those left on board

*Men Of Issachar*

could not be saved. This appeal secured the accomplishment of the promise. So God's telling the elect that if they apostatize they shall perish, prevents their apostasy. And in like manner, the Bible teaching that those for whom Christ died shall perish if they violate their conscience, prevents their transgressing, or brings them to repentance. God's purposes embrace the means as well as the end. If the means fail, the end will fail. He secures the end by securing the means. It is just as certain that those for whom Christ died shall be saved, as that the elect shall be saved. Yet in both cases the event is spoken of as conditional. There is not only a possibility, but an absolute certainty of their perishing if they fall away. But this is precisely what God has promised to prevent. This passage, therefore, is perfectly consistent with those numerous passages which teach that Christ's death secures the salvation of all those who were given to him in the covenant of redemption (Charles Hodge, *Commentary On The First Epistle To The Corinthians*).

In other words, the warning serves to turn the elect away from the peril. Therefore, the warning (against causing a little one to fall away from the faith) concerns a very real possibility that can only be avoided through the sovereign grace of Almighty God. Those who would presume upon this grace and do things to cause a little one to perish have shown by their behavior (if they remain unrepentant) that they themselves were never born again.

In the final analysis these things go beyond the realm of human understanding. Our tendency is to diminish the urgency of Christ's words, claiming that someone who is truly born-again will not fall away regardless of what another person may do. But that is not how Jesus presented the situation. He

## Kingdom Status

wants us to think of this circumstance in a certain way. We're supposed to have the mind of Christ on this issue and accept the idea that ungodly behavior has the potential of destroying one who is in Christ. Any attempt to qualify these words of Jesus apart from the teaching of God's word is a show of arrogance and stupidity.

According to Christ scandalizing behavior is so serious that it impacts the entire world. The term he uses is *kosmos* and that normally refers to all of creation. It can sometimes refer to all the people who live on earth but in this case I believe he is referring the created realm. These words remind us that sin touches every part of the universe. Moreover, this particular sin has an impact that ripples throughout all of creation. There is a butter-fly effect when those who are in relation to Jesus Christ are brutalized to the point that their eternal destiny is in doubt. This is contrary to the kingdom way. A person in relationship with Jesus Christ cannot lose their salvation and the whole world is shaken when a member of the King's household is thrust into apostasy.

Furthermore, the person who causes this type of stumbling reveals their own sinful character. They reveal pride, arrogance and every evil way that have not been purged by a relationship with Jesus. They do not exhibit Christ and so we can say with some confidence that they are not part of the kingdom of God. They have not been changed by the power of the Word and they have not embraced Jesus Christ as their master and Savior.

Unfortunately, scandalizing will come; this is something of a mystery. Why does God allows this to happen? Part of the reason is that God uses the

*Men Of Issachar*

unregenerate to sharpen and strengthen his children. God has determined his purposes will be accomplished by humans and that means there will be plenty of error mixed in with the good. Not only that, God's purpose is accomplished even by the sinful acts of man. The crucifixion of Jesus Christ is an example. Through sinful behavior, God's perfect will was accomplished. This certainly doesn't mean the one causing scandal is without guilt. Instead, it reveals their character and, unless there is repentance, it reveals that they are not part of the kingdom of God.

It is such an important issue that Christ uses some very startling language to instruct his apostles concerning what they should do to make sure they are not guilty of scandalizing a little one. He tells his apostles it would be better to be maimed than to be cast into everlasting fire. He is not saying they should literally cut off a hand or foot in order to purge themselves of pride and self-centeredness. He is telling them they must deal very aggressively with the un-Christlike attitudes that lead to scandalizing behavior.

Practically speaking, what does Jesus have in mind? It could be a number of things but primarily it would be a prideful attitude that sneers at a little one and considers him of no consequence. In short, anything we do that would hamper the humble behavior of a childlike Christian needs to be dealt with in a violent and aggressive manner. Not physical violence but a violence of conviction. A violence that does not spare oneself. A violence that realizes the need to do away with the impression of the old man. It is a violence that understands the need to walk in obedience to God's Word at all costs. In Psalm 119 it says, *How can a young man cleanse his way? By taking heed according to Your word. With my whole heart I have sought You; Oh, let me not wander from Your commandments! Your word I have hidden in my heart, That I might not sin against You* (Psalms 119:9-11). This is the way we "amputate" a hand or foot or "gouge out" an eye in the kingdom of heaven. Not literally but by striving in the strength of the Holy Spirit to walk in obedience to God's Word. Not literally but by laboring to overcome sinful desire and behavior. This is why we need to *know* God's Word. This is why the apostles needed to know Scripture in light of Jesus Christ's life and ministry. A life of obedience to the Word of God requires great effort in the strength of the Holy Spirit. Thus, Jesus is calling his disciples to a radical commitment.

The alternative is hellfire. A person not willing to do what is necessary to gain the attitude of a little one is not truly born-again. I think this is another example of a warning designed to turn the elect away from a peril. Those who hear this warning and heed it are those who are truly in Christ. Those who recognize the need to rid themselves of the impression of the old man with all of its arrogance and self-centeredness, will look to the Word of God as the standard for their behavior and do all they can to live accordingly.

This is very strong language. Jesus is talking about eternal damnation. Indeed, it is probably the strongest reference to eternal punishment found in the New Testament.

I don't want you to think Jesus is telling his apostles there is no hope for those who cause a scandal. And remember, when I use the term scandal I am simply making use of the Greek term and I am

*Men Of Issachar*

talking about behavior which causes a little one to fall away from the faith. Jesus is speaking of a real danger when he confronts his apostles with this teaching. He is saying, in some way, it is truly possible to destroy the faith of a little one. It is all the more terrible when scandalizing behavior comes from a fellow Christian. This behavior may result from a lack of understanding but it is rebellion nonetheless.

This portion of Scripture is often used to teach us about mild examples of "scandalizing" another person. We are told that Jesus has in mind is a circumstance in mind where a fellow Christian causes a little one to sin in some fashion. Moreover, we are often told the "little one" is literally a child. The idea that this discourse is concerned with mild scandal is fine as far as it goes. That kind of scandal is real. That kind of scandal can be exemplified in the foolish behavior of a believer toward a fellow Christian which causes them to do something they should not do.

However, Jesus Christ has much more in mind. The circumstance he is speaking of is far more severe. He is speaking of Christians who cause a fellow believer to fall away from the faith. Nevertheless, there is hope.

### *Must Be Retrieved*

It seems odd to say someone can fall away from the faith and yet come back; it appears the scandal is not such a big deal after all. But that is not what Jesus says. He tells us the fall into ruin is very real. He says it is such an important matter that the person who causes this fall should be dealt with severely and if a person recognizes an attitude within himself leading to this, he should do something very

*Kingdom Status*

dramatic to rid himself of it.

Having described the danger a little one faces when confronted with an arrogant Christian, Jesus realizes the apostles might be thinking it would be better if these "little ones" just went away and left them alone. The apostles are probably feeling rather scornful toward the little ones and Jesus wants to correct that as well. He does not want his apostles to consider little ones as beneath them and more trouble than they're worth. He does not want little ones to be ridiculed, ignored or badmouthed simply because they don't measure up to the world's standards.

Jesus says the little ones are under God's special care but he is not saying every Christian - or every child - has a personal guardian angel. The Bible tells us angels are in the service of God and given the duty to watch over God's people. Many people use this passage to build an entire doctrine of angels and their place in God's economy. Entire books have been written suggesting angels are available to everyone as personal guardians, charged to protect, guide and represent us. However, angels do not represent us before God and this passage does not teach that every Believer has a personal guardian angel. Jesus is simply telling his apostles that the little ones - those who are true believers - are watched over by angels in a general sense.

After all, the Son of Man came to save what was lost. The Son of Man is the one who restores humanity to its proper place in God's system. I think Jesus referred to himself as the Son of Man at this point for a reason. He is reminding his apostles he is greater than the angels and wants them to remember *he* represents little ones.

Thus, he uses the example of a shepherd and his sheep. Throughout the Old Testament this metaphor is used to describe God's relationship with his people. Likewise, Jesus calls himself the shepherd of the sheep and the good Shepherd. And in this illustration, Jesus says the life of a single little one who is lost is of such great importance, he will bend every effort to retrieve that lost lamb.

There is such rejoicing when this lost sheep is found because eternity is in the balance. Eternity in that this little one's life is in jeopardy and the entire fabric of the messianic reign is under stress. For Jesus made it very plain that, *My sheep hear My voice, and I know them, and they follow Me. And I give them eternal life, and they shall never perish; neither shall anyone snatch them out of My hand. My Father, who has given them to Me, is greater than all; and no one is able to snatch them out of My Father's hand* (John 10:27-29). In other words, once saved always saved.

So, what do we make of this? Jesus is emphatic about the eternal security of those who are born again. Why then this great concern over a little one who has wandered away? The reason is that much can happen to a sheep that has left the fold. If it truly is a "little one" then it will not be eternally lost; a true little one cannot perish but they *can* be badly injured and scarred. Moreover, there will be those who have every evidence of being a "little one" and are identified as such, yet because of the pride and arrogance of another Christian, they *will* leave the faith. Even though they were not genuinely born again, the one who drives them away will be held responsible for their eternal damnation. Jesus is telling his apostles that the person who causes a little one to be scandalized will pay a heavy price even though a true believer will eventually be brought back into the fold. If they are truly saved they are always saved. However, someone "has to die" to pay for the crime and that someone would be the person who caused a believer to fall away - even if that fall is temporary.

Because this is true, every effort must be made to retrieve any Christian who wanders from the faith. It is of vital importance they be brought back. The integrity of the kingdom depends upon it. The good word of the good Shepherd depends upon it.

## *Conclusion*

Are you a "little one?" Are you small in your own eyes? Are you a Believer, having placed faith in Jesus Christ alone for salvation? Do you understand that in the kingdom of God there is no place for a concern about status? To be a little one has nothing to do with age or physical size but has everything to do with your relationship with Jesus Christ and your imitation of him. None of us are going to be perfect but all of us must strive to have the mind that is in Christ Jesus. As the apostle Paul wrote to the church in Philippi, *Let nothing be done through selfish ambition or conceit, but in lowliness of mind let each esteem others better than himself. Let each of you look out not only for his own interests, but also for the interests of others* (Philippians 2:3-4). This is the essence of the "little one." It is to think of others more highly than yourself. It is to recognize the servant, the one who takes the lowly place, pleases the Lord Jesus Christ the most. So, is this what you strive for; to be a little one, to reject self-esteem in favor of esteeming others, indeed, in favor of Christ esteem?

Furthermore, how do you feel about "little

*Men Of Issachar*

ones?" Do you esteem others who exhibit the character of a servant? One of the ways to prove your esteem of little ones is by imitating them. If you seek to be little, find someone to watch who exudes the character of Christ so you may copy them.

Understand, being little does not somehow exempt you from exercising proper authority or from taking dominion in your arena of activity. To be meek, little and humble before the Lord does not mean you are Harvey Milquetoast. It means you get things done as a leader through service. You do what you do in order to serve other people and thereby serve the Lord and bring glory to his name. It means you do not draw attention to yourself. And you stand firm for truth without trying to make a name for yourself.

I should also ask if you *promote* littleness. To do so you need to understand what it means to be little in the kingdom of God. You need to understand how this plays into your duty to cultivate the new creation and to manifest the reign of Jesus Christ in your sphere of influence. This requires mindful Christian living. We cannot coast through life and hope for the best. Too many Christians are satisfied with arriving on time for the Sunday service or some other "churchy" behavior. That will not do. To promote littleness is to understand your place in the kingdom of God and work to manifest the reign of Jesus Christ in *everything* you do. And you cannot do that if you don't give plenty of thought to what it means to be little and yet a servant *leader*. Certain kinds of leadership, by the way, are for every Christian. All of us lead in some fashion. I've focused on men of Christ in this book but the fact is, every Christian needs to be a leader in their arena of

## Kingdom Status

activity in one fashion or another. This is because a Christian must show others how a person can live a life of "littleness" while they serve and promote the authority of Jesus Christ.

I must also ask if you scandalize little ones? A common way this occurs is through a failure to esteem the humble, servant-like members of the body. As mentioned, this passage applies to "mild" forms of scandalizing as well as "full blown" scandalizing. It might be a lack of esteem on your part that causes a brother or sister to stumble; they may react to your arrogance in a way that is not Christlike. For instance, suppose a parent is doing their best to raise their child in the fear and admonition of the Lord by word and deed. Yet, the child rebels and shows contempt for the parent. It may cause the parent to stumble. They might relax their vigilance and cease to exemplify Christlike behavior. Or perhaps they respond in a way that is prideful or arrogant to the rebellious behavior of the child. That is one way a Christian might cause a "little one" to stumble. The irony in this example is that the little one is the parent rather than the child.

Furthermore, I ask if you protect little ones? This means you encourage and nurture those who exhibit faith in Jesus Christ and help them along the path of righteousness. You protect fellow Believers who are humble and striving to be servants in the messianic kingdom. You do this even as you act little yourself.

Thus, you need to protect your own "littleness" as well. You need to feed an attitude of humility and Christlike servant behavior. You cannot do that if you are stuffing yourself full of worldliness.

Do not forget that Jesus was teaching his

apostles about the ultimate scandal when he told them if they caused a little one to fall away from the faith they would be liable to the most severe punishment. I hope none of you are guilty of this but if you are, recognize it and take action. Even as you do so, your concern should be for the other person rather than yourself. True, the assurance of your own salvation hangs in the balance but that is the case with the person you have caused to stumble as well. If you are a true believer, if you *are* born again, then you will have concern for the other person first. Paul exemplifies this attitude when he says, *for I could wish that I myself were cursed from Christ for my brethren, my countrymen according to the flesh* (Romans 9:3). The context is different but the attitude is the same. Paul is as concerned with the eternal state of others as he is with his own. This may be hyperbole on the part of Paul, but my emphasis is that a follower of Jesus Christ will place others before himself.

If you have caused a little one to stumble to the point that they have fallen away from the faith, do everything within your power to retrieve them. An example of this is when a parent drives their child away from the faith by their un-Christlike behavior. While most young children will naturally follow the example of their parents in seeking Christ, that early inclination may be thwarted by a poor example and a child may fall away from the faith. If you have experienced that, I entreat you, do whatever you can to rectify the problem. You don't know if God will use you to bring your child back into the fold but it is very important to do all you can to accomplish that. As I mentioned earlier, the very fabric of the kingdom of God is placed under stress when this

*Kingdom Status*

happens. I'm not saying the kingdom will somehow fall if you fail to reclaim a lost little one; I *am* saying you yourself will experience a great stress on your walk with the Lord Jesus Christ. Again, if you are repentant and seeking the face of Almighty God it's not a matter of your salvation being in jeopardy or that you were never born again; I am saying you will experience tremendous pain and stress in your life because of it - all the more so if the lost little one is your own child.

Thus, in a very real sense, you will be accountable for the loss of a little one if you do not repent of that sin and do not do what you can to bring them back to the faith. Certainly they carry personal responsibility but it would be wrong to walk away from the damage we have done without bending every effort to undo the harm.

Not all who walk away from the faith are little ones. Some are scandalized by truth. Indeed, the Scripture tells us many folks were scandalized by Jesus. However, we do not have the privilege of deciding who has been scandalized by truth or who has stumbled due to our foolish behavior. So the bottom line is that if we feel we have been guilty of causing a little one to fall away, it is our duty to seek the one who has been lost in order to bring them back to Jesus Christ.

Christ wants all of God's children to be little ones, to be unconcerned with status. We must cultivate the mind of Christ so we can understand kingdom reality and comprehend how to manifest that actuality in this realm. It is easy for us to *say* "the last shall be first" in the kingdom or to *say* the servant is the most esteemed - but we often *act* differently when the rubber meets the road. All of us

*Men Of Issachar*

must lay down our lives for others just as Jesus Christ laid his life down for us. This is truly honorable behavior. This kind of lifestyle will win for us a leading role in the kingdom of God.

Furthermore, we must watch over one another and encourage one another in the task of becoming "more little." This is part of our service to fellow Christians and we cannot neglect it.

Finally, if you have caused a little one to stumble, I urge you to do all in your power to retrieve them. Doing so will reassure you of *your* standing as a little one and by God's grace you will be used to seek and to save that which was lost. May God be so merciful to us.

# ADDENDUM
## PRELIMINARY WORLDVIEW READING LIST

**History**
*Kingdom of Priests: A History of Old Testament Israel*, by Eugene H. Merrill
*The Temple*, by Alfred Edershiem
*New Testament History*, by F. F. Bruce
*Wars Of The Jews*, by Flavius Josephus
*The Story Of Christianity*, by Justo Gonzales
*A History Of Christianity: I & II*, by Kenneth Scott Latourette
*How the Irish Saved Civilization*, by Thomas Cahill
*The Great Christian Revolution*, by Otto Scott
*James: Fool As King*, by Otto Scott
*Robespierre: Fool As Revolutionary*, by Otto Scott
*Worldly Saints*, by Leland Ryken
*The Puritan Hope*, by Ian Murray
*The Secret Six*, by Otto Scott
*Revival and Revivalism*, by Ian Murray
*History of the American People*, by Paul Johnson
*Modern Times*, by Paul Johnson
*Leftism Revisited*, by Eric von Kuehnelt-Leddihn
*The Politically Incorrect Guide to American History*, by Thomas E. Woods Jr.
*A Theological Interpretation of American History*, by C. Gregg Singer

# Theology
*Biblical Hermeneutics*, by Milton S. Terry
*Let The Reader Understand*, by Dan McCartney and Charles Clayton
*The Structure Of Biblical Authority*, by Meridith G. Kline
*That You May Prosper*, by Ray Sutton
*Introduction to Systematic Theology*, by Cornelius van Till
*The Book Of Leviticus, NICOT*, by Gordon J. Wenham
*The Book Of Deuteronomy, NICOT*, by Peter Craigie
*The Epistle To The Romans, NICNT*, by Douglas Moo
*The Epistle To The Galatians, NICNT*, by Ronald Y.K. Fung
*The Institutes of the Christian Religion*, by John Calvin
*The Institutes of Biblical Law*, by R. J. Rushdoony
*Systematic Theology*, by Louis Berkhof
*The Defense of the Faith*, by Cornelius van Till
*A Christian View of Men and Things*, by Gordon Clark
*Predestination*, by Gordon Clark
*Through New Eyes*, by James Jordan
*The Parousia*, by J. Stuart Russell
*Paradise Restored*, by David Chilton
*The Days Of Vengeance*, by David Chilton
*Heretics,* by G. K. Chesterton
*Orthodoxy*, by G.K. Chesterton
*Everlasting Man*, by G.K. Chesterton
*The Pursuit of Holiness*, by Jerry Bridges
*The Practice of Godliness*, by Jerry Bridges
*The Way of Life*, by Charles Hodges
*75 Questions*, by Gary North
*Total Truth*, by Nancy Pearcey
*Culture In Christian Perspective*, by Leland Ryken
*Joy Unspeakable*, by Martyn Lloyd-Jones
*The Kingdom Of God*, by Martyn Lloyd-Jones

*Shine Forth As The Sun: The Messianic Reign In Parable According To Matthew's Gospel*, by D. Eric Williams
*Real Faith: Studies in the Epistle of James*, by D. Eric Williams

**Science**
*Politically Incorrect Guide To Science*, by Tom Bethel
*Darwin's Black Box*, by Michael Behe
*Evolution: Theory in Crisis*, by Michael Denton
*Nature's Destiny*, by Michael Denton
*Defeating Darwinism by Opening Minds*, by Philip Johnson
*The Philosophical Scientists*, by David Foster
*Is The World Running Down?*, by Gary North

**Economics**
*Productive Christians in an age of Guilt Manipulators*, by David Chilton
*The Politically Incorrect Guide to The Great Depression and The New Deal*, by Robert P. Murphy
*The Politically Incorrect Guide to Capitalism*, by Robert P. Murphy
*The Sinai Strategy: Economics And the Ten Commandments*, by Gary North
*Tools of Dominion: The Case Laws Of Exodus*, by Gary North
*The Alpha Strategy*, by John Pugsley
*Politics of Guilt and Pity*, by R. J. Rushdoony
*The Ultimate Resource 2*, by Julian Simon

**Education**
*Is Public Education Necessary?,* by Samuel Bluemenfeld
*Tyranny Through Public Education*, by William F. Cox Jr.
*The Christian Philosophy of Education*, by Gordon Clark

*The Philosophy of The Christian Curriculum*, by R. J. Rushdoony
*Education, Christianity and the state*, by Gresham Machen
*The Children Trap*, by Robert Thoburn
*Dumbing Us Down*, by John Taylor Gatto
*The Messianic Character Of American Education*, by R. J. Rushdoony
*An Underground History of American Education*, by John Taylor Gatto
*Weapons Of Mass Instruction*, by John Taylor Gatto

D. Eric Williams has ministered throughout the Mountain-West region of the United States since 1988. He holds a BA from the University of the State of New York an MA from the Southern California Graduate School of Theology and is ordained with the Conservative Congregational Christian Conference. Eric, his wife and nine children have homeschooled for over 20 years.

# Real Faith
## Studies In The Epistle Of James
ISBN/EAN13: 1441436782 / 9781441436788
Page Count: 174

The Epistle of James is all about Faith - real faith, living faith, active faith. Like the apostle Paul, James would have us work out our salvation with fear and trembling. This book endeavors to show how that is done.

According to James' epistle, real faith is based upon certain presuppositions. True faith finds joy in hardship. Faith brings unity in the body; it engenders self control; it benefits the individual and the world at large.

*Real Faith, Studies In The Epistle Of James* will en-able you to read the letter of James with fresh eyes and allow you to apply this misunderstood book to your walk of faith.

*I am happy to commend D. Eric Williams' studies in the epistle of James. "Real Faith" is down-to-earth, just like the epistle, and is well-suited to help the reader unpack the kind of practical help that James is known for.* Douglas Wilson

# The End Was Near
End Times Bible Prophecy Made Simple
ISBN/EAN13: 1451591209 / 9781451591200
Page Count: 140

Are we living in the Last Days? Are the End Times upon us? Many popular writers confidently say we are the terminal generation - but is that what the Bible says? Find out in this introductory study of biblical eschatology by Pastor and writer D. Eric Williams.

In this brief overview of the topic, Pastor Williams reveals the proper approach to interpreting End Time passages and provides the tools necessary for understanding biblical eschatology.

# Shine Forth As The Sun
## The Messianic Reign In Parable According To Matthew's Gospel
ISBN/EAN13: 144143772X / 9781441437723
Page Count: 225

The kingdom of God: when will it begin? What are its characteristics? Who will be a part of it? Drawing from the "kingdom is like" parables of our Lord Jesus Christ, Pastor D. Eric Williams examines these questions and more in this collection of sermons concerning the kingdom of God according to Matthew's Gospel.

# Also By D. Eric Williams

**The Christmas Season**
Stories For Each Week of Advent
And Christmas Eve
ISBN/EAN13: 1434816575 / 9781434816573
Page Count: 100

**The Power Presentation**
Career Acceleration Through Public Speaking
ISBN/EAN13: 1434818985 / 9781434818980
Page Count: 150

**Quasimodo On Skis**
A Collection Of Humorous Essays Designed to Produce A Chuckle In Even The Most Curmudgeonly Of People
ISBN /EAN 13: 1460931971 / 978-1460931974
Page Count: 101

Printed in Great Britain
by Amazon